CAMBRIDGE SCHOOL

Shakespeare

King John

Edited by Pat Baldwin and Rex Gibson

Series Editor: Rex Gibson
Director, Shakespeare and Schools Project

CAMBRIDGE
UNIVERSITY PRESS

Published by the Press Syndicate of the University of Cambridge
The Pitt Building, Trumpington Street, Cambridge CB2 1RP
40 West 20th Street, New York, NY 10011–4211, USA
10 Stamford Road, Oakleigh, Melbourne 3166, Australia

First published 1994
Printed in Great Britain at the University Press, Cambridge

A catalogue record for this book is available from the British Library.

Library of Congress cataloging in publication data applied for

ISBN 0 521 44582 5 paperback

Prepared for publication by Stenton Associates
Designed by Richard Morris, Stonesfield Design
Picture research by Callie Kendall

Thanks are due to the following for permission to reproduce photographs:

Front cover: 'King John Stag Hunting' by permisssion of the British Library, London,
Cotton, Claudius, D2, folio 116; Dürer, 'Four Horsemen of the Apocalypse', reproduced
by permission of the Syndics of the Cambridge University Library. 18, 50, 60, 97*t*, 116,
135*tc*, 136*l*, 156, Angus McBean; 20, courtesy of the Henry E. Huntington Library, San
Marino, California; 21, 44, 57, 66, 67, 97*b*, 104, 128, 135*b*, 136*r*, 152, 166, Donald Cooper
© Photostage; 22, courtesy of the Folger Shakespeare Library; 22 (inset), courtesy of office
de Tourisme, Angiers; 30, Gunther Dietel/Deutsches Nationaltheater Weimar; 56, from
William Tyr's *History of the Crusades* in *Runciman: The First Crusade*, Cambridge University
Press, 1980/reproduced courtesy of the Syndics of the Cambridge University Library; 78,
Mander & Mitchenson Theatre Collection; 88, 135*tr*, Tom Holte Collection/Shakespeare
Centre Library, Stratford-upon-Avon; 135*tl*, Shakespeare Centre Library, Stratford-
upon-Avon/photo: Ernest Daniels; 148, Imperial War Museum, London; 173, Joe Cocks
Studio Collection/Shakespeare Centre Library, Stratford-upon-Avon.

Contents

Cambridge School Shakespeare

This edition of *King John* is part of the *Cambridge School Shakespeare* series. Like every other play in the series, it has been specially prepared to help all students in schools and colleges.

This *King John* aims to be different from other editions of the play. It invites you to bring the play to life in your classroom, hall or drama studio through enjoyable activities that will increase your understanding. Actors have created their different interpretations of the play over the centuries. Similarly, you are encouraged to make up your own mind about *King John*, rather than having someone else's interpretation handed down to you.

Cambridge School Shakespeare does not offer you a cut-down or simplified version of the play. This is Shakespeare's language, filled with imaginative possibilities. You will find on every left-hand page: a summary of the action, an explanation of unfamiliar words, a choice of activities on Shakespeare's language, characters and stories.

Between each act and in the pages at the end of the play, you will find notes, illustrations and activities. This will help to increase your understanding of the whole play.

There is a large number of activities to give you the widest choice to suit your own particular needs. Please don't think you have to do every one. Choose the activities that will help you most.

This edition will be of value to you whether you are studying for an examination, reading for pleasure, or thinking of putting on the play to entertain others. You can work on the activities on your own or in groups. Many of the activities suggest a particular group size, but don't be afraid to make up larger or smaller groups to suit your own purposes.

Although you are invited to treat *King John* as a play, you don't need special dramatic or theatrical skills to do the activities. By choosing your activities, and by exploring and experimenting, you can make your own interpretations of Shakespeare's language, characters and stories. Whatever you do, remember that Shakespeare wrote his plays to be acted, watched and enjoyed.

Rex Gibson

This edition of *King John* uses the text of the play established by L. A. Beaurline in *The New Cambridge Shakespeare*.

List of characters

England

KING JOHN
QUEEN ELEANOR his mother
PRINCE HENRY his son
BLANCHE his niece

PEMBROKE
SALISBURY
ESSEX
BIGOT
} English Barons

THE BASTARD Philip Falconbridge, illegitimate son of
  King Richard (Cœur-de-lion)
LADY FALCONBRIDGE his mother
ROBERT FALCONBRIDGE his half-brother
JAMES GURNEY servant to Lady Falconbridge
HUBERT
ENGLISH HERALD
MESSENGER

PETER OF POMFRET a prophet
EXECUTIONERS

France

KING PHILIP
LEWIS his son, the Dauphin
ARTHUR Duke of Brittany, nephew of John and
  claimant to his throne
CONSTANCE his mother
DUKE OF AUSTRIA Viscount of Limoges
MELUN A French Lord
CHATILLON Ambassador to England
CITIZEN of Angiers
FRENCH HERALD
MESSENGER

Emissary of the Pope

PANDULPH Cardinal and Papal legate

Lords, a Sheriff, soldiers, trumpeters, attendants,
other citizens of Angiers

The action of the play takes place in England and in France.

The Angevin Empire

King John's father, King Henry II, was the founder of the Angevin dynasty which ruled England from 1154 to 1485. The Angevins, who first ruled in Anjou, came to be better known by their nickname 'Plantagenet', after the sprig of broom (from Old French, *plante genêt*) they wore in their caps. The family was also called 'the Devil's Brood' because they were always fighting each other. For example, three of Henry's sons (Henry, Richard and John) all rebelled against him, in attempts to seize territory.

Through marriage to Eleanor of Aquitaine, diplomacy and conquest, King Henry II acquired a huge empire. It stretched from the border with Scotland to the Pyrenees (see map opposite). The empire was under constant attack by King Philip II of France. During John's reign, nearly all the Angevin continental territories were lost to Philip.

Shakespeare's play begins shortly after John has succeeded to the throne. King Richard I (Cœur-de-lion) has just died, and John has inherited the Angevin Empire. Philip, determined to expand his own territory, sides with Arthur, the son of John's older brother, Geoffrey. The French ambassador demands that John surrender all his lands and titles to Arthur. John rejects the claim. But his legal position is weak, as this family tree suggests:

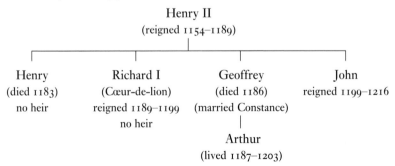

Henry II
(reigned 1154–1189)

Henry	Richard I	Geoffrey	John
(died 1183)	(Cœur-de-lion)	(died 1186)	reigned 1199–1216
no heir	reigned 1189–1199	(married Constance)	
	no heir		

Arthur
(lived 1187–1203)

At this time, England respected the custom of male primogeniture, whereby the father's title and estates were inherited by the eldest son or his heirs. Arthur therefore seems to have had a better claim to the throne of England than John. But, on his deathbed, Richard I had made a will making John his rightful heir.

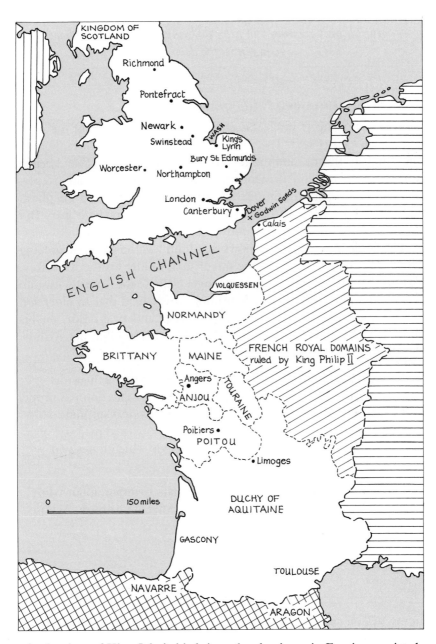

At the time of King John's birth in 1167, the Angevin Empire consisted of all the unshaded territory. King Philip's rule was only secure in a fairly small region around Paris (the Ile de France). But by the time John died in 1216, Philip controlled almost all the land that is modern France.

The ambassador of France demands that John
give all his territories and titles to Arthur, or war will follow.
John rejects the demand.

---

1 'Borrowed majesty?' (in groups of three)

Lines 1–43 abruptly pitch the audience into the politics of the play.
King Richard I (Cœur-de-lion) has just died, and John has inherited
the English throne and huge territories in France. The French
ambassador, Chatillon, demands that King John surrender all his titles
and lands (the Angevin Empire, see pages 2 and 3) to John's nephew,
Arthur. John rejects the claim and threatens immediate war. But
Eleanor reveals (line 40) that John's legal position is weak.

The family tree on page 2 shows that John was the youngest of King
Henry II's sons. Arthur was the son of John's older brother Geoffrey.
Arthur therefore seems to have a stronger claim to the Angevin Empire
than John. The custom of male primogeniture held that an older son
(or his son) must inherit his father's lands and titles. But, on his
deathbed, Richard I had made a will which made John, not Arthur,
heir to the Angevin Empire.

a Take parts as John, Chatillon and Eleanor. Experiment with
  different ways of speaking lines 1–43. For example, John as proud
  or weak and uncertain; Chatillon as courteous or insulting;
  Eleanor as angry or fearful (will she snap 'borrowed majesty' or
  whisper it?). After your explorations, decide which tones you
  think are most appropriate.

b Turn to the family tree on page 2, and talk together about who
  you think had the stronger claim to the Angevin Empire, Arthur
  or John.

In my behaviour through me
borrowed stolen, usurped
embassy message
sways usurpingly rules illegally

proud control fierce compulsion
Controlment for control force
  for force

The Tragedy of King John

ACT 1 SCENE 1
London King John's palace

Enter KING JOHN, QUEEN ELEANOR, PEMBROKE, ESSEX, SALISBURY,
attendants and CHATILLON *of France*

KING JOHN Now say, Chatillon, what would France with us?
CHATILLON Thus, after greeting, speaks the King of France
  In my behaviour to the majesty,
  The borrowed majesty of England here.
ELEANOR A strange beginning: 'borrowed majesty'?   5
KING JOHN Silence, good mother, hear the embassy.
CHATILLON Philip of France, in right and true behalf
  Of thy deceasèd brother Geoffrey's son,
  Arthur Plantagenet, lays most lawful claim
  To this fair island and the territories,   10
  To Ireland, Poitiers, Anjou, Touraine, Maine,
  Desiring thee to lay aside the sword
  Which sways usurpingly these several titles,
  And put the same into young Arthur's hand,
  Thy nephew and right royal sovereign.   15
KING JOHN What follows if we disallow of this?
CHATILLON The proud control of fierce and bloody war,
  To enforce these rights so forcibly withheld.
KING JOHN Here have we war for war and blood for blood,
  Controlment for control. So answer France.   20
CHATILLON Then take my king's defiance from my mouth,
  The farthest limit of my embassy.

John threatens instant invasion of France. Eleanor blames Constance for stirring up trouble, but secretly acknowledges Arthur's stronger legal right. The Bastard brings a dispute for judgement by John.

1 Shakespeare's mistake?

King John says in line 26, 'The thunder of my cannon shall be heard'. But cannons did not exist in John's time! Gunpowder was not invented until one hundred years later. Like the clock that Shakespeare put into *Julius Caesar*, this is an anachronism: including something in a play or story about the past which, in fact, belongs to a later age.

But does it matter? Imagine you are giving a lecture on *King John*. One of your students interrupts, saying, 'Shakespeare made a mistake here, didn't he?'. What do you reply?

2 Possession or right? (in pairs)

In line 40, Eleanor reminds King John that his claim to the throne is weak. She stresses that his 'possession' is stronger than his lawful claim ('right'). It's like the proverb, 'Possession is nine-tenths of the law': if you already possess something, you have a stronger chance of holding on to it.

Talk together about how you think John reacts when he hears his mother speak line 40. At this early point in the play, would you wish to present him as fully confident of his right, or would you wish to show his unease about his claim to England's crown?

3 Making the Church pay

King John orders that the Church must pay the expenses of the war (lines 48–9). As you read on, you will find that this is one of several causes of tension between John and the Church.

---

ere before
sullen presage gloomy foreteller, dismal prophet
honourable conduct dignified escort, safe conduct
kindled stirred up
right and party claim and cause

manage governments
issue outcome (and pun on 'children')
liege lord
expedition's charge war's expense
Cœur-de-lion King Richard I (the Lionheart)

KING JOHN Bear mine to him, and so depart in peace.
    Be thou as lightning in the eyes of France;
    For ere thou canst report, I will be there: 25
    The thunder of my cannon shall be heard.
    So hence. Be thou the trumpet of our wrath,
    And sullen presage of your own decay.
    An honourable conduct let him have.
    Pembroke, look to't. Farewell, Chatillon.   30
                        Exeunt Chatillon and Pembroke
ELEANOR [*Whispers*] What now, my son, have I not ever said
    How that ambitious Constance would not cease
    Till she had kindled France and all the world
    Upon the right and party of her son?
    This might have been prevented and made whole   35
    With very easy arguments of love,
    Which now the manage of two kingdoms must
    With fearful-bloody issue arbitrate.
KING JOHN Our strong possession and our right for us.
ELEANOR Your strong possession much more than your right,   40
    Or else it must go wrong with you and me;
    So much my conscience whispers in your ear,
    Which none but heaven and you and I shall hear.

            Enter a sheriff [and whispers Essex in the ear]

ESSEX My liege, here is the strangest controversy
    Come from the country to be judged by you   45
    That e'er I heard. Shall I produce the men?
KING JOHN Let them approach.
                                        [*Exit sheriff*]
    Our abbeys and our priories shall pay
    This expedition's charge.

Enter ROBERT FALCONBRIDGE *and Philip [the* BASTARD *with sheriff]*

                    What men are you?
BASTARD Your faithful subject I, a gentleman,   50
    Born in Northamptonshire, and eldest son,
    As I suppose, to Robert Falconbridge,
    A soldier, by the honour-giving hand
    Of Cœur-de-lion, knighted in the field.

In the inheritance dispute, the Bastard says he and his brother have the same mother, but he doubts they have the same father. Eleanor and John detect similarities to Richard Cœur-de-lion in the Bastard.

1 Robert versus the Bastard

King John finds himself judging a case that has parallels to his own position. Who is the legal heir to a father's lands? John's right to the throne of England and the Angevin Empire is challenged by Arthur, the son of John's elder brother. Now Robert Falconbridge disputes the right of his older brother, the Bastard, to inherit the family estate. Primogeniture (see page 2) is again questioned.

Before you turn the page, guess who you think John will favour: the Bastard or Robert. There may be a clue in the way in which John addresses Robert in line 90.

2 The Bastard (in pairs)

To help you gain a first impression of the Bastard's personality, try these activities:

a One partner reads aloud everything the Bastard says opposite. The other echoes every time he refers to himself ('I', 'my', 'mine').

b Speak the last line of each speech as ironically or humorously as you can (lines 63, 70 and 83).

c Speak the lines in several different ways: trying to make every line pleasantly humorous; angrily; with mock innocence.

d 'Perfect Richard.' Eleanor and King John agree that the Bastard resembles Richard Cœur-de-lion, the great warrior king (lines 85–90). Suggest five words of your own to describe the Bastard's physical appearance.

---

put you o'er refer you
diffidence mistrust
a pops me out he swindles me
whe'er ... true begot whether I'm
  as legitimate
well begot handsome

Fair fall the bones may my father
  rest in peace
mad-cap comedian
trick characteristic, trait
large composition huge size,
  general manner

KING JOHN What art thou?   55
ROBERT The son and heir to that same Falconbridge.
KING JOHN Is that the elder, and art thou the heir?
   You came not of one mother then, it seems.
BASTARD Most certain of one mother, mighty king –
   That is well known – and as I think one father.   60
   But for certain knowledge of that truth
   I put you o'er to heaven, and to my mother.
   Of that I doubt, as all men's children may.
ELEANOR Out on thee, rude man! Thou dost shame thy mother,
   And wound her honour with this diffidence.   65
BASTARD I, madam? No, I have no reason for it.
   That is my brother's plea, and none of mine,
   The which if he can prove, a pops me out
   At least from fair five hundred pound a year.
   Heaven guard my mother's honour, and my land!   70
KING JOHN A good blunt fellow. Why being younger born
   Doth he lay claim to thine inheritance?
BASTARD I know not why, except to get the land,
   But once he slandered me with bastardy.
   Now whe'er I be as true begot or no,   75
   That still I lay upon my mother's head,
   But that I am as well begot, my liege –
   Fair fall the bones that took the pains for me –
   Compare our faces and be judge yourself.
   If old Sir Robert did beget us both   80
   And were our father and this son like him,
   O old Sir Robert, father, on my knee
   I give heaven thanks I was not like to thee!
KING JOHN Why, what a mad-cap hath heaven lent us here!
ELEANOR He hath a trick of Cœur-de-lion's face,   85
   The accent of his tongue affecteth him.
   Do you not read some tokens of my son
   In the large composition of this man?
KING JOHN Mine eye hath well examinèd his parts
   And finds them perfect Richard. [*To Robert*] Sirrah, speak,   90
   What doth move you to claim your brother's land?

Robert Falconbridge claims that the Bastard is really Richard's son. Robert says his father's will made him the sole heir. But John rejects the validity of old Sir Robert's deathbed will.

1 Who's who? Point it out! (in groups of six)

Robert Falconbridge tells his story to support his claim to his father's land. Richard Cœur-de-lion had sent Robert's father (old Sir Robert) on an important mission to Germany. In Sir Robert's absence, King Richard seduced his wife, resulting in the birth of Philip (the Bastard). On his deathbed, Sir Robert disowned the Bastard, and left all his lands to his younger son, Robert. But King John rejects Robert's claim, and decides in favour of the Bastard.

Take parts as Robert, the Bastard, old Sir Robert, Sir Robert's wife, King John and Richard Cœur-de-lion. Sit in a circle. Read aloud lines 95–129, (one person reading every part, if you wish). As each character is mentioned, everyone points emphatically to that person. For example, in line 95 there are four possible pointing actions: 'My' (point to Robert), 'gracious liege' (point to King John), 'my' (point to Robert), and 'father' (point to old Sir Robert).

You will find that this activity will help your understanding of who's who in this case of primogeniture.

2 Legal parallel?

On his deathbed, Richard Cœur-de-lion left the Angevin Empire to John, his youngest brother (rather than to Arthur, son of Geoffrey, who was next in line to the throne after Richard). Sir Robert also made a deathbed will, but King John overrules it.

Draw a Falconbridge family tree to show the nature of the inheritance dispute. Compare it with the family tree on page 2.

---

half-face profile, thin face
face cheek
groat thin silver coin
employed seduced
treat of high affairs negotiate on important issues

sojourned stayed
got conceived
wedlock marriage
play false deceive
In sooth in truth
get conceive

BASTARD Because he hath a half-face like my father!
    With half that face would he have all my land –
    A half-faced groat five hundred pound a year!
ROBERT My gracious liege, when that my father lived,   95
    Your brother did employ my father much –
BASTARD [*Aside*] Well sir, by this you cannot get my land:
    Your tale must be how he employed my mother.
ROBERT And once dispatched him in an embassy
    To Germany, there with the emperor   100
    To treat of high affairs touching that time.
    Th'advantage of his absence took the king,
    And in the meantime sojourned at my father's,
    Where how he did prevail I shame to speak.
    But truth is truth. Large lengths of seas and shores 105
    Between my father and my mother lay,
    As I have heard my father speak himself,
    When this same lusty gentleman was got.
    Upon his deathbed he by will bequeathed
    His lands to me, and took it on his death   110
    That this my mother's son was none of his;
    And if he were, he came into the world
    Full fourteen weeks before the course of time.
    Then, good my liege, let me have what is mine,
    My father's land, as was my father's will.   115
KING JOHN Sirrah, your brother is legitimate:
    Your father's wife did after wedlock bear him,
    And if she did play false, the fault was hers,
    Which fault lies on the hazards of all husbands
    That marry wives. Tell me, how if my brother, 120
    Who as you say took pains to get this son,
    Had of your father claimed this son for his?
    In sooth, good friend, your father might have kept
    This calf, bred from his cow, from all the world;
    In sooth he might. Then if he were my brother's, 125
    My brother might not claim him, nor your father,
    Being none of his, refuse him. This concludes:
    My mother's son did get your father's heir,
    Your father's heir must have your father's land.

*Eleanor offers the Bastard a choice: the Falconbridge lands or honour as
Richard's son. The Bastard instantly chooses honour, and gives the
Falconbridge lands to Robert. The Bastard is knighted by John.*

'Look where three-farthings goes!'
(lines 142–3).
An Elizabethan three-farthings coin
showed a rose behind the head of
Queen Elizabeth I.

1 Thin actor, or dirty joke?

Some people believe that Shakespeare wrote the part of Robert
Falconbridge for John Sinklo, a very thin actor. It is thought that his
appearance would give extra amusement to audiences, as they heard
the Bastard speak lines 138–47. Another point of view on the lines
is that they are loaded with sexual innuendo, as Elizabethans would
recognise sexual double meanings in 'shape', 'riding-rods', 'eel-skins',
'stuffed', 'stir', 'foot', 'Sir Nob' and 'case'.

Imagine you are directing the play. An actor tells you about these
two possibilities and asks, 'Should we try to let the audience know
anything about these two points of view?'. What do you reply?

2 'Arise Sir Richard'

A stage version of the ceremony is shown on page 21. Work out how
you would stage lines 161–2. Would you make it a simple ritual, or a
very elaborate theatrical ceremony?

Whether ... be which would you
rather be
reputed acknowledged, known
Lord of thy presence your own
man

riding-rods horse whips (or thin
switches)
durst dare
country manners ... way
ordinary country folk usually give
way to more important people

ROBERT   Shall then my father's will be of no force   130
        To dispossess that child which is not his?
BASTARD   Of no more force to dispossess me, sir,
        Than was his will to get me, as I think.
ELEANOR   Whether hadst thou rather be: a Falconbridge,
        And like thy brother to enjoy thy land,   135
        Or the reputed son of Cœur-de-lion,
        Lord of thy presence and no land beside?
BASTARD   Madam, and if my brother had my shape
        And I had his, Sir Robert's his, like him,
        And if my legs were two such riding-rods,   140
        My arms such eel-skins stuffed, my face so thin
        That in mine ear I durst not stick a rose
        Lest men should say 'Look where three-farthings goes!'
        And to his shape were heir to all this land,
        Would I might never stir from off this place,   145
        I would give it every foot to have this face.
        I would not be Sir Nob in any case.
ELEANOR   I like thee well. Wilt thou forsake thy fortune,
        Bequeath thy land to him, and follow me?
        I am a soldier and now bound to France.   150
BASTARD   Brother, take you my land, I'll take my chance.
        Your face hath got five hundred pound a year,
        Yet sell your face for five pence and 'tis dear.
        Madam, I'll follow you unto the death.
ELEANOR   Nay, I would have you go before me thither.   155
BASTARD   Our country manners give our betters way.
KING JOHN   What is thy name?
BASTARD   Philip, my liege, so is my name begun,
        Philip, good old Sir Robert's wife's eldest son.
KING JOHN   From henceforth bear his name whose form thou
             bearest: 160
        Kneel thou down Philip, but rise more great,
        Arise Sir Richard and Plantagenet.
BASTARD   Brother by th'mother's side, give me your hand;
        My father gave me honour, yours gave land.
        Now blessèd be the hour by night or day   165
        When I was got, Sir Robert was away.

The Bastard acknowledges that he is illegitimate. John confirms Robert Falconbridge's inheritance. The Bastard reflects on his new-found honour and mocks such newly-created knights.

1 Proverbs

The Bastard's lines 170–5 contain proverbs, well known in Elizabethan times. They all hint at his illegitimate birth:

line 170 'from the right': heraldic term denoting a bastard
line 171 popular phrases for children born outside marriage
line 172 night-walkers = prostitutes
line 173 possession is important, irrespective of birth
line 174 hints at Richard Cœur-de-lion's sexual conquest ('well shot')
line 175 I am myself, bastardy doesn't matter.

Imagine that the director of a stage production advises King John to react to one of the Bastard's lines in a way which shows that he recognises his own dubious right to the crown. Which line would you choose, and why?

2 Promotion makes you forget your friends?

'For new-made honour doth forget men's names', says the Bastard at line 187. He means that as you gain promotion and status, you put on airs and graces, like pretending you can't remember people's names. Do you think that this is true?

3 'Like an Absey book'

The Bastard mockingly imagines how he will talk with other knights at his dinner table ('my worship's mess'). His pretentious conversation will be like 'an Absey book' (an ABC book, used to teach reading by question and answer). Try speaking lines 192–204 using a deliberately affected voice for the dialogue.

---

grandam grandmother
landless knight the Bastard
landed squire gentleman landowner
Good den God give you good evening
respective polite

conversion newly-honoured knight
traveller important visitor
toothpick (suggesting affected behaviour)
sufficed filled
catechise question
pickèd man selected, tooth-picker

ELEANOR The very spirit of Plantagenet.
         I am thy grandam, Richard, call me so.
BASTARD Madam, by chance but not by truth; what though?
         Something above a little from the right,   170
             In at the window, or else o'er the hatch.
         Who dares not stir by day must walk by night,
             And have is have, however men do catch.
         Near or far off, well won is still well shot,
             And I am I, howe'er I was begot.   175
KING JOHN Go, Falconbridge, now hast thou thy desire;
         A landless knight makes thee a landed squire.
         Come madam, and come Richard, we must speed
         For France, for France, for it is more than need.
BASTARD Brother adieu, good fortune come to thee,   180
         For thou wast got i'th'way of honesty.
                              Exeunt all but Bastard
         A foot of honour better than I was,
         But many a many foot of land the worse.
         Well, now can I make any Joan a lady.
         'Good den, Sir Richard.' – 'Godamercy fellow.'   185
         And if his name be George, I'll call him Peter;
         For new-made honour doth forget men's names:
         'Tis too respective and too sociable
         For your conversion. Now your traveller,
         He and his toothpick at my worship's mess,   190
         And when my knightly stomach is sufficed,
         Why then I suck my teeth and catechise
         My pickèd man of countries: 'My dear sir',
         Thus leaning on mine elbow I begin,
         'I shall beseech you' – that is Question now,   195
         And then comes Answer like an Absey book:
         'O sir', says Answer, 'at your best command,
         At your employment, at your service, sir.'
         'No sir', says Question, 'I, sweet sir, at yours.'
         And so e'er Answer knows what Question would,   200
         Saving in dialogue of compliment,
         And talking of the Alps and Apennines,
         The Pyrenean and the river Po,
         It draws toward supper in conclusion so.

The Bastard decides to practise flattery, to aid his promotion and to avoid being tricked. His mother arrives, seeking her younger son. The Bastard says he knows her husband was not his father.

1 The Bastard's soliloquy

Lines 182–216 are a soliloquy: spoken by an actor who is alone on stage (or believes he or she is alone), and showing the character's true thoughts. Use the following sections to advise the actor how to speak the soliloquy line by line:

lines 182–3	I have a title but no land
line 184	Any woman I marry will become a lady
lines 185–9	I'll be condescending to my social inferiors
lines 189–204	I can entertain who I choose and have pretentious conversations with them about foreign parts
lines 205–9	Ambitious people must learn to flatter
lines 210–13	So I'll flatter to impress others – because I really want to
lines 214–16	My flattery will help me not to be tricked by others, and will help my social promotion.

2 James Gurney: sole appearance

This is James Gurney's one appearance in the play, and he speaks only four words (line 231). 'Philip' was a popular name for a sparrow in Elizabethan times. Decide whether you think the Bastard is joking with James Gurney, or is sharply telling him off for being so familiar.

3 Colbrand the Giant

The Bastard's lines 224–6 mock his half-brother, Robert. Colbrand the Giant was a legendary Danish hero. Turn back to lines 138–47 to remind yourself of what the Bastard really thinks of Robert.

---

mounting spirit ambitious person
smack of observation practise
  flattery
habit and device dress and symbol
accoutrement clothing
inward motion inner desire
sweet poison flattery

woman-post female messenger
holds in chase hunts
toys trifles, gifts (knighthoods)
Sir Robert ... fast there's nothing
  of Sir Robert in me
marry indeed

But this is worshipful society,   205
And fits the mounting spirit like myself;
For he is but a bastard to the time
That doth not smack of observation,
And so am I – whether I smack or no,
And not alone in habit and device,   210
Exterior form, outward accoutrement,
But from the inward motion – to deliver
Sweet, sweet, sweet poison for the age's tooth,
Which, though I will not practise to deceive,
Yet to avoid deceit, I mean to learn,   215
For it shall strew the footsteps of my rising.
But who comes in such haste in riding-robes?
What woman-post is this? Hath she no husband
That will take pains to blow a horn before her?

Enter LADY FALCONBRIDGE *and* JAMES GURNEY

O me, 'tis my mother. How now, good lady?   220
What brings you here to court so hastily?
LADY FALCONBRIDGE Where is that slave, thy brother? Where is he
That holds in chase mine honour up and down?
BASTARD My brother Robert, old Sir Robert's son?
Colbrand the Giant, that same mighty man?   225
Is it Sir Robert's son that you seek so?
LADY FALCONBRIDGE Sir Robert's son. Ay, thou unreverend boy,
Sir Robert's son! Why scorn'st thou at Sir Robert?
He is Sir Robert's son, and so art thou.
BASTARD James Gurney, wilt thou give us leave a while?   230
GURNEY Good leave, good Philip.
BASTARD   Philip? – sparrow! James,
There's toys abroad; anon I'll tell thee more.
                                  Exit James [*Gurney*]
Madam, I was not old Sir Robert's son.
Sir Robert might have eat his part in me
Upon Good Friday and ne'er broke his fast.   235
Sir Robert could do well – marry, to confess –
Could he get me. Sir Robert could not do it.
We know his handiwork. Therefore, good mother,

17

Lady Falconbridge reveals that Richard Cœur-de-lion was the Bastard's father. Richard would not take no for an answer. The Bastard is delighted, and says his mother's seduction was unavoidable and no sin.

Truth will out. Lady Falconbridge tells her son the truth at last: he is the son of Richard Cœur-de-lion.

1 'Basilisco-like'

The exchange between the Bastard and his mother in lines 243–4 echoes an Elizabethan play of 1591–2. Basilisco was a boastful character who referred to himself as 'Knight, knight'. His servant mocked him with 'knave, knave'.

beholding indebted	**issue** child
holp helped	**get** be conceived
untoward unmannerly, rude	**privilege** excusing
Basilisco a boastful knight in an Elizabethan play	**at his dispose** to use as he wished
dubbed knighted	**Subjected tribute** gift from a subject or subordinate
vehement suit passionate courtship	

To whom am I beholding for these limbs?
Sir Robert never holp to make this leg.   240
LADY FALCONBRIDGE Hast thou conspirèd with thy brother too,
  That for thine own gain shouldst defend mine honour?
  What means this scorn, thou most untoward knave?
BASTARD Knight, knight, good mother, Basilisco-like.
  What, I am dubbed, I have it on my shoulder.   245
  But mother, I am not Sir Robert's son,
  I have disclaimed Sir Robert and my land;
  Legitimation, name, and all is gone.
  Then, good my mother, let me know my father –
  Some proper man I hope. Who was it, mother?   250
LADY FALCONBRIDGE Hast thou denied thyself a Falconbridge?
BASTARD As faithfully as I deny the devil.
LADY FALCONBRIDGE King Richard Cœur-de-lion was thy father.
  By long and vehement suit I was seduced
  To make room for him in my husband's bed.   255
  Heaven! lay not my transgression to my charge
  That art the issue of my dear offence,
  Which was so strongly urged past my defence.
BASTARD Now by this light, were I to get again,
  Madam, I would not wish a better father.   260
  Some sins do bear their privilege on earth,
  And so doth yours: your fault was not your folly,
  Needs must you lay your heart at his dispose,
  Subjected tribute to commanding love,
  Against whose fury and unmatchèd force   265
  The aweless lion could not wage the fight,
  Nor keep his princely heart from Richard's hand.
  He that perforce robs lions of their hearts
  May easily win a woman's. Ay, my mother,
  With all my heart I thank thee for my father.   270
  Who lives and dares but say thou didst not well
  When I was got, I'll send his soul to hell.
  Come, lady, I will show thee to my kin,
   And they shall say, when Richard me begot,
  If thou hadst said him nay, it had been sin.   27.
  Who says it was, he lies; I say 'twas not.
         Exeunt

Looking back at Act 1

Activities for groups or individuals

1 Family matters (in pairs)

Act 1 is much concerned with questions of inheritance. King John's right to succeed his brother as king is mirrored in the Falconbridge dispute: which brother should inherit his father's land? Shakespeare loads the act with 'family' words ('father', 'brother', 'son', 'mother', and so on).

a Choose any two pages at random. Identify all the 'family' words and suggest how they illustrate the theme of inheritance.

b Turn to page 11. One person reads aloud the whole page. The other echoes every 'family' word.

2 Sons and mothers

Two pairs of sons and mothers appear in Act 1: King John and Eleanor, and the Bastard and Lady Falconbridge. Make a list of the ways in which the mothers resemble or differ from each other. Suggest the feelings of each mother towards her son.

Richard Cœur-de-lion. This woodcut of 1530 illustrates a popular legend. King Richard tore the heart out of a lion that was attacking him (Cœur-de-lion = heart of a lion). The legend is mentioned in Act 1 Scene 1, lines 266–7 (see also page 57).

'Arise Sir Richard and Plantagenet.'
King John creates the Bastard a knight.

3 The Bastard

'Bastard' is a word that was used for a child born outside marriage. For centuries, the word was used as an insult and carried a social stigma. Today, it is still used as an insult, but often without its original meaning, because attitudes to such children have changed enormously. In the play, Philip Falconbridge is called 'the Bastard' to describe his social position.

One student said, 'I don't feel comfortable with the word. Can't we call him something else?'. What would you reply?

4 'Borrowed majesty'

The play is much concerned with whether King John is a usurper: someone who has illegally seized the throne. As you read through the play, look out for each time the word 'usurp' is used in some way or other. You will find that, as well as direct challenges to John's right to rule, there is much indirect questioning of his authority.

5 Honour: different meanings?

Consider, in turn, each character who appears in Act 1. Write a sentence for each, to express what he or she understands by 'honour'.

King Philip welcomes the Duke of Austria, killer of Richard Cœur-de-lion, to aid Arthur in battle against John. Arthur also welcomes Austria, who vows strong support against England.

The scene shifts from England to France. In the nineteenth century, elaborate sets were used to depict the city of Angiers (*Angers*, in French). The city was part of King John's Angevin inheritance (see page 2). These illustrations show how Angiers was portrayed in William Charles Macready's production in 1842, and (inset) the actual medieval city walls (built shortly after John's time). Design your own set for Act 2.

---

forerunner ancestor
robbed the lion (see page 20)
holy wars in Palestine the
 Crusades
importance bidding, request
spread his colours fight
 (colours = flags)

usurpation illegal seizure of the
 throne
The rather that as soon as
indenture pledge, contract
pale fence
foot coast
coops encloses, protects
main sea

ACT 2   SCENE 1
Outside the walls of Angiers

Enter from one side, the DUKE of AUSTRIA and his forces.
From the other side, enter KING PHILIP, LEWIS the DAUPHIN,
CONSTANCE, ARTHUR and their forces

KING PHILIP [*Embraces Austria*] Before Angiers well met, brave
    Austria. –

    Arthur, that great forerunner of thy blood,
    Richard, that robbed the lion of his heart
    And fought the holy wars in Palestine,
    By this brave duke came early to his grave,   5
    And for amends to his posterity,
    At our importance hither is he come
    To spread his colours, boy, in thy behalf,
    And to rebuke the usurpation
    Of thy unnatural uncle, English John.   10
    Embrace him, love him, give him welcome hither.
ARTHUR God shall forgive you Cœur-de-lion's death
    The rather that you give his offspring life,
    Shadowing their right under your wings of war.
    I give you welcome with a powerless hand   15
    But with a heart full of unstainèd love.
    Welcome before the gates of Angiers, duke.
KING PHILIP A noble boy! Who would not do thee right?
AUSTRIA Upon thy cheek lay I this zealous kiss
    As seal to this indenture of my love: 20
    That to my home I will no more return
    Till Angiers and the right thou hast in France,
    Together with that pale, that white-faced shore,
    Whose foot spurns back the ocean's roaring tides
    And coops from other lands her islanders,   25
    Even till that England, hedged in with the main –

King Philip proposes an attack on Angiers, but Constance, thinking John may have agreed peace, urges delay. Chatillon, hampered by bad weather, brings news: John comes to fight.

1 Praise or sarcasm?

In Shakespeare's *King Richard II*, John of Gaunt praises England's strength as an island (Act 2 Scene 1, lines 46–63):

> This precious stone set in the silver sea
> Which serves it in the office of a wall
> Or as a moat defensive to a house …
> England, bound in with the triumphant sea
> Whose rocky shore beats back the envious siege
> Of watery Neptune, …

Gaunt is an Englishman, so his patriotic speech is understandable. Yet Austria, an enemy of England, also seems to praise the 'water-wallèd bulwark'. But does he speak lines 23–8 sarcastically, admiringly or in some other way? Read Austria's lines aloud several times, in different tones of voice. Decide how you think he should speak.

2 Peace or war? (in pairs)

Constance talks about the possibility of peace. One person reads lines 32–61, while the other echoes all the words to do with love and peace. Change over, but this time echo the words which suggest war. Which are there more of, 'war' words or 'peace' words? Talk together about what your discovery suggests about the mood of the scene.

3 'To cull the plots of best advantages'

King Philip's order (line 40) could mean either 'destroy the strongest positions in Angiers', or 'choose the best positions from which to attack'. Do you think one makes better sense than the other, or are both interpretations possible?

---

bulwark fortress
purposes attacks, plots
follow arms go to war
more requital a greater show
cannon (see page 6)

Stay wait
coldly calmly, unemotionally
paltry unimportant
leisure ceasing
expedient to rapidly approaching

That water-wallèd bulwark, still secure
And confident from foreign purposes –
Even till that utmost corner of the west
Salute thee for her king. Till then, fair boy,   30
Will I not think of home but follow arms.

CONSTANCE   O take his mother's thanks, a widow's thanks,
Till your strong hand shall help to give him strength
To make a more requital to your love.

AUSTRIA   The peace of heaven is theirs that lift their swords   35
In such a just and charitable war.

KING PHILIP   Well then, to work; our cannon shall be bent
Against the brows of this resisting town.
Call for our chiefest men of discipline
To cull the plots of best advantages.   40
We'll lay before this town our royal bones,
Wade to the market-place in Frenchmen's blood,
But we will make it subject to this boy.

CONSTANCE   Stay for an answer to your embassy,
Lest unadvised you stain your swords with blood;   45
My Lord Chatillon may from England bring
That right in peace which here we urge in war,
And then we shall repent each drop of blood
That hot rash haste so indirectly shed.

Enter CHATILLON

KING PHILIP   A wonder, lady! Lo, upon thy wish   50
Our messenger Chatillon is arrived.
What England says, say briefly, gentle lord;
We coldly pause for thee. Chatillon, speak.

CHATILLON   Then turn your forces from this paltry siege
And stir them up against a mightier task: 55
England, impatient of your just demands,
Hath put himself in arms. The adverse winds,
Whose leisure I have stayed, have given him time
To land his legions all as soon as I.
His marches are expedient to this town,   60
His forces strong, his soldiers confident.

Chatillon tells of the arrival of the powerful English forces, eager to fight. John claims he has the right to enter Angiers, and threatens war. King Philip claims that Arthur has the greater right.

1 Mercenary soldiers (in pairs)

Many of the soldiers in the English army are mercenaries: young men who fight for payment and excitement. Such people, who will fight for any cause for money and thrills, are found in every age. In lines 66–72, Chatillon describes these soldiers of fortune with a mixture of praise and blame. He admires them as a 'braver choice of dauntless spirits' (line 72), but also describes them as 'Rash, inconsiderate' (line 67).

Invent a dialogue between two modern mercenaries, which explains where and why they are fighting, and how they justify their actions. Try to make them as much like King John's soldiers as possible.

2 King or country? (in groups of six)

Throughout the play, the words 'France' and 'England' can refer to either the country or the king, or both. In line 91, 'England' refers to either King John or Arthur. Take parts as France (the king), France (the country), England (the king), England (the country) and Arthur. The sixth person slowly reads lines 84–95. If you think you are being referred to, raise your hand. If no one (or more than one person) puts their hand up, talk together about whom you think is being mentioned.

Ate Greek goddess of discord	**waft o'er** brought over
the king's deceased the dead king (Cœur-de-lion)	**To do offence and scathe** to attack and ravage
unsettled humours discontented men	**churlish** harsh
ladies' faces hairless, young	**circumstance** detail
spleens hot tempers	**parley** talk, negotiate
bottoms ships	**lineal** legitimate
	underwrought undermined

With him along is come the mother-queen,
An Ate stirring him to blood and strife;
With her her niece, the Lady Blanche of Spain;
With them a bastard of the king's deceased;   65
And all th'unsettled humours of the land –
Rash, inconsiderate, fiery voluntaries,
With ladies' faces and fierce dragons' spleens –
Have sold their fortunes at their native homes,
Bearing their birthrights proudly on their backs,   70
To make a hazard of new fortunes here.
In brief, a braver choice of dauntless spirits
Than now the English bottoms have waft o'er
Did never float upon the swelling tide
To do offence and scathe in Christendom.   75
                    Drum beats
The interruption of their churlish drums
Cuts off more circumstance: they are at hand,
To parley or to fight, therefore prepare.
KING PHILIP How much unlooked for is this expedition.
AUSTRIA By how much unexpected, by so much   80
                    We must awake endeavour for defence,
                    For courage mounteth with occasion.
                    Let them be welcome then; we are prepared.

Enter KING JOHN, BASTARD, QUEEN ELEANOR, BLANCHE,
    PEMBROKE, SALISBURY *and the English army*

KING JOHN Peace be to France, if France in peace permit
                    Our just and lineal entrance to our own.   85
                    If not, bleed France, and peace ascend to heaven,
                    Whiles we, God's wrathful agent, do correct
                    Their proud contempt that beats his peace to heaven.
KING PHILIP Peace be to England, if that war return
                    From France to England, there to live in peace. 90
                    England we love, and for that England's sake
                    With burden of our armour here we sweat.
                    This toil of ours should be a work of thine;
                    But thou from loving England art so far
                    That thou hast underwrought his lawful king,   95

King Philip accuses John of seizing England's crown, which is Arthur's by God's authority. Eleanor accuses Constance of wishing to dominate the world. The two women exchange insults.

1 Who's who? (in groups of four)

Three people take parts as King John, Geoffrey and Arthur. The fourth person slowly reads lines 99–109. As each character is mentioned, everyone points emphatically to that person.

2 Be a lawyer

Both King Philip and King John use many legal words when they make their cases:

'abstract' = a précis of a long piece of legal writing

'brief' = a document that contains all the points of law needed by a lawyer for a case

'commission' = the authority given to a lawyer to represent a client

'articles' = a legal document

'warrant' = legal authorisation

'impeach' = to accuse of a crime against the state, usually treason.

Imagine an actor says to you, 'In the theatre, nearly every member of the audience simply won't *get* the significance of all these legal words. Why does it matter that we, the actors, should know their meaning?' Make your reply.

3 Double insult: who's a queen? (in pairs)

The word 'queen' (line 123) could also mean 'whore'. Take parts as Eleanor and Constance. Read lines 121–33, making Constance's reaction to the insult, and the women's reactions to each other, as clear as possible. Physical actions might be useful!

---

sequence of posterity heirs
Outfacèd infant state defied childhood
abstract essence (Arthur)
owe owns

o'ermasterest hold, possess
supernal judge God
check rule (the image is from chess)
and if even if
blots slanders

Cut off the sequence of posterity,
Outfacèd infant state, and done a rape
Upon the maiden virtue of the crown.
Look here upon thy brother Geoffrey's face.
These eyes, these brows, were moulded out of his;   100
This little abstract doth contain that large
Which died in Geoffrey, and the hand of time
Shall draw this brief into as huge a volume.
That Geoffrey was thy elder brother born,
And this his son, England was Geoffrey's right,   105
And this is Geoffrey's. In the name of God
How comes it then that thou art called a king,
When living blood doth in these temples beat
Which owe the crown that thou o'ermasterest?
KING JOHN   From whom hast thou this great commission, France,   110
    To draw my answer from thy articles?
KING PHILIP   From that supernal judge that stirs good thoughts
    In any breast of strong authority
    To look into the blots and stains of right.
    That judge hath made me guardian to this boy,   115
    Under whose warrant I impeach thy wrong,
    And by whose help I mean to chastise it.
KING JOHN   Alack, thou dost usurp authority.
KING PHILIP   Excuse it is to beat usurping down.
ELEANOR   Who is it thou dost call usurper, France?   120
CONSTANCE   Let me make answer: thy usurping son.
ELEANOR   Out, insolent! Thy bastard shall be king
    That thou mayst be a queen and check the world!
CONSTANCE   My bed was ever to thy son as true
    As thine was to thy husband, and this boy   125
    Liker in feature to his father Geoffrey
    Than thou and John in manners, being as like
    As rain to water or devil to his dam.
    My boy a bastard! By my soul, I think
    His father never was so true begot.   130
    It cannot be, and if thou wert his mother.
ELEANOR   There's a good mother, boy, that blots thy father.
CONSTANCE   There's a good grandam, boy, that would blot thee.

The Bastard insults Austria over Richard Cœur-de-lion's death.
King Philip claims John's territories for Arthur. John demands that
Arthur submit to him. Eleanor and Constance argue and Arthur weeps.

'Good my mother, peace.' Arthur weeps, and is comforted by Constance,
as the two women trade insults. From a German production of *King John*
in Weimar, 1980.

1 King John?

Why do you think that King Philip addresses John as 'King John' at
line 151? It is at a moment when he demands that John surrender his
army and lands to Arthur. In so doing, Philip denies that John is the
legal king.

Hear the crier! (criers called for
silence in a court of law)
And a may catch your hide if he
seizes your lion-skin
smoke beat
well did he become it suited him
well

Alcides Hercules (famous Greek
hero)
cracker boaster
Brittaine Brittany
coil turmoil

AUSTRIA Peace!

BASTARD   Hear the crier!

AUSTRIA   What the devil art thou?

BASTARD One that will play the devil, sir, with you,   135
    And a may catch your hide and you alone.
    You are the hare of whom the proverb goes,
    Whose valour plucks dead lions by the beard;
    I'll smoke your skin-coat and I catch you right.
    Sirrah, look to't! I'faith I will, i'faith.   140

BLANCHE O, well did he become that lion's robe
    That did disrobe the lion of that robe.

BASTARD It lies as sightly on the back of him
    As great Alcides' shoes upon an ass.
    But ass, I'll take that burden from your back   145
    Or lay on that shall make your shoulders crack.

AUSTRIA What cracker is this same that deafs our ears
    With this abundance of superfluous breath?
    King Philip, determine what we shall do straight.

KING PHILIP Women and fools, break off your conference.   150
    King John, this is the very sum of all:
    England and Ireland, Anjou, Touraine, Maine,
    In right of Arthur do I claim of thee.
    Wilt thou resign them and lay down thy arms?

KING JOHN My life as soon. I do defy thee, France.   155
    Arthur of Brittaine, yield thee to my hand,
    And out of my dear love I'll give thee more
    Than e'er the coward hand of France can win.
    Submit thee, boy.

ELEANOR   Come to thy grandam, child.

CONSTANCE Do, child, go to it grandam, child.   160
    Give grandam kingdom, and it grandam will
    Give it a plum, a cherry, and a fig.
    There's a good grandam.

ARTHUR   Good my mother, peace.
    I would that I were low laid in my grave.
    I am not worth this coil that's made for me.   165

ELEANOR His mother shames him so, poor boy, he weeps.

Constance accuses Eleanor of being responsible for Arthur's grief, because Arthur is being punished for Eleanor's sins. King Philip quietens the women and summons the citizens of Angiers.

1 Eleanor versus Constance (in pairs)

The two women continue to insult each other, using Arthur as a pawn in their argument. Take parts as Eleanor and Constance. Read lines 159–94, but ignore Arthur's and King John's lines. Experiment with different ways of speaking. For example, is Eleanor commanding, wheedling or loving? Is Constance sarcastic, mocking or angry? After your explorations, work on one or two of the following:

a Didn't you say that before?

Constance often repeats her points. Arthur's tears are mentioned twice ('heaven-moving pearls' in line 169, and 'crystal beads' in line 171). Find other examples of the same words being repeated.

b Why all the Ws?

Eleanor's mention of 'A will' (line 192) provokes Constance to a great deal of alliteration (using words beginning with the same letter). She uses 'will' both in the sense of a legal document disposing of a dead person's possessions, and as meaning desire or motive. Speak Constance's lines 193–4, emphasising the Ws, then work out the meaning of each of the four uses of 'will'.

c 'Eldest son's son'

Constance's line 177 could mean 'eldest grandson' (Arthur), or it could be an 'overclaim', creating the impression that Arthur is the son of King Richard I. Which do you think is most likely?

---

dominations possessions
The canon of the law the guilt of
  previous generations
Bedlam lunatic
her sin King John
beadle court officer who whips
  offenders

cankered diseased, corrupted
temperate calm
this presence those people
  present, my royal presence
to cry aim to encourage (like
  supporters in an archery contest)

CONSTANCE Now shame upon you, whe'er she does or no!
          His grandam's wrongs, and not his mother's shames,
          Draws those heaven-moving pearls from his poor eyes,
          Which heaven shall take in nature of a fee.   170
          Ay, with these crystal beads heaven shall be bribed
          To do him justice and revenge on you.
ELEANOR Thou monstrous slanderer of heaven and earth!
CONSTANCE Thou monstrous injurer of heaven and earth,
          Call not me slanderer! Thou and thine usurp   175
          The dominations, royalties, and rights
          Of this oppressèd boy. This is thy eldest son's son,
          Infortunate in nothing but in thee.
          Thy sins are visited in this poor child,
          The canon of the law is laid on him,   180
          Being but the second generation
          Removèd from thy sin-conceiving womb.
KING JOHN Bedlam, have done.
CONSTANCE   I have but this to say,
          That he is not only plaguèd for her sin,
          But God hath made her sin and her the plague   185
          On this removèd issue, plagued for her
          And with her plague; her sin his injury,
          Her injury, the beadle to her sin,
          All punished in the person of this child,
          And all for her. A plague upon her!   190
ELEANOR Thou unadvisèd scold, I can produce
          A will that bars the title of thy son.
CONSTANCE Ay, who doubts that? a will, a wicked will,
          A woman's will, a cankered grandam's will.
KING PHILIP Peace, lady; pause or be more temperate,   195
          It ill beseems this presence to cry aim
          To these ill-tunèd repetitions.
          Some trumpet summon hither to the walls
          These men of Angiers. Let us hear them speak
          Whose title they admit, Arthur's or John's.   200
                        Trumpet sounds

          Enter a CITIZEN [*and others*] *upon the walls*

CITIZEN Who is it that hath warned us to the walls?

John and King Philip address the citizens of Angiers. John speaks first and claims that, if he had not made haste, the French would not be talking to the citizens, but destroying Angiers.

1 A sleeping city (in pairs)

King John uses a great deal of personification (see page 182). Angiers is compared to a person asleep; the cannons have 'bowels' and 'spit' indignantly.

One person slowly reads lines 207–28. The partner echoes every personified word: the first is 'eye' in line 208. Afterwards, talk together about the power of such personification in creating an image of the city as vulnerable as the human body. You will meet many other examples of personification as you read on.

2 'Bullets' or 'words'?

King John tells the citizens of Angiers that the French have changed their tactics (lines 226–30). Instead of threatening with the violence of 'bullets' (cannon balls), they offer 'a parle' (negotiation), in which 'calm words' are 'folded up in smoke' (breath).

Draw a picture of the choice that John says is being offered to Angiers.

3 Safety in a storm (in pairs)

King John uses the word 'harbourage' (a safe port for boats) in line 234. Talk together about the comparison John is making here, and suggest why it may have extra appeal to the citizens of Angiers.

---

advantage benefit, opportunity
compulsion of their ordinance
  force of their cannons
of lime made of limestone
dishabited dislodged, undressed
expedient speedy

amazed fearful
vouchsafe suggest
faithless error mistake against
  your vows
Forewearied exhausted

KING PHILIP 'Tis France, for England.
KING JOHN   England for itself.
    You men of Angiers, and my loving subjects –
KING PHILIP You loving men of Angiers, Arthur's subjects,
    Our trumpet called you to this gentle parle –   205
KING JOHN For our advantage; therefore hear us first.
    These flags of France, that are advancèd here
    Before the eye and prospect of your town,
    Have hither marched to your endamagement.
    The cannons have their bowels full of wrath,   210
    And ready mounted are they to spit forth
    Their iron indignation 'gainst your walls.
    All preparation for a bloody siege
    And merciless proceeding by these French
    Confronts your city's eyes, your winking gates;   215
    And but for our approach, those sleeping stones,
    That as a waist doth girdle you about,
    By the compulsion of their ordinance
    By this time from their fixèd beds of lime
    Had been dishabited, and wide havoc made   220
    For bloody power to rush upon your peace.
    But on the sight of us your lawful king,
    Who painfully with much expedient march
    Have brought a countercheck before your gates,
    To save unscratched your city's threatened cheeks,   225
    Behold, the French amazed vouchsafe a parle,
    And now, instead of bullets wrapped in fire
    To make a shaking fever in your walls,
    They shoot but calm words folded up in smoke,
    To make a faithless error in your ears,   230
    Which trust accordingly, kind citizens,
    And let us in, your king, whose laboured spirits,
    Forewearied in this action of swift speed,
    Craves harbourage within your city walls.

King Philip claims that Angiers belongs to Arthur. If the citizens accept the claim, Philip's army will leave. If not, Angiers will be attacked. The Citizen refuses entry to both kings.

1 The power of persuasion (in pairs)

King John and King Philip use high-flown, rhetorical language (see page 186). Both wish to persuade the citizens of Angiers of the strength and right of their claims. Choose one of the following activities:

a Find the substance of each argument

Identify the four main sections of each king's argument (lines 206–34 and lines 235–66).

b Who has the stronger case?

Who do you think makes the stronger case? Do they answer each other's arguments or ignore them?

c The power of presentation

Explore ways to test the theory that the way you speak is more important than what you actually say. First, speak John and Philip's lines rhetorically, that is, don't worry about the *meaning*, just try to make the words sound as impressive as possible. Second, try to make the meaning clear in a number of ways, for example, by speaking conversationally, sorrowfully, or in a philosophical, reasoned way.

After your explorations, advise the actors about how you think they should deliver the lines.

d Actions speak louder?

Line 236 suggests that Philip is holding the hand of Arthur. This is clever diplomacy and a strong visual image. Work out the gestures and movements that Philip might make in lines 236–48, to use the presence of Arthur to the greatest effect.

---

upon to uphold
that he enjoys his possessions
down-trodden equity oppressed right
hospitable zeal friendly enthusiasm, zealous aid
owes has right to

Save in aspect only in appearance
sealed up excused
unvexed retire peaceful retreat
fondly pass stupidly ignore
roundure circle
messengers of war cannon balls
discipline military skill

KING PHILIP When I have said, make answer to us both.   235
       Lo, in this right hand, whose protection
       Is most divinely vowed upon the right
       Of him it holds, stands young Plantagenet,
       Son to the elder brother of this man,
       And king o'er him and all that he enjoys.   240
       For this down-trodden equity we tread
       In warlike march these greens before your town,
       Being no further enemy to you
       Than the constraint of hospitable zeal,
       In the relief of this oppressèd child,   245
       Religiously provokes. Be pleasèd then
       To pay that duty which you truly owe
       To him that owes it, namely, this young prince,
       And then our arms, like to a muzzled bear,
       Save in aspect, hath all offence sealed up.   250
       Our cannons' malice vainly shall be spent
       Against th'invulnerable clouds of heaven,
       And with a blessèd and unvexed retire,
       With unhacked swords and helmets all unbruised,
       We will bear home that lusty blood again,   255
       Which here we came to spout against your town,
       And leave your children, wives, and you in peace.
       But if you fondly pass our proffered offer,
       'Tis not the roundure of your old-faced walls
       Can hide you from our messengers of war,   260
       Though all these English and their discipline
       Were harboured in their rude circumference.
       Then tell us, shall your city call us lord
       In that behalf which we have challenged it?
       Or shall we give the signal to our rage   265
       And stalk in blood to our possession?
CITIZEN In brief, we are the King of England's subjects;
       From him and in his right we hold this town.
KING JOHN Acknowledge then the king, and let me in.
CITIZEN That can we not, but he that proves the king,   270
       To him will we prove loyal. Till that time
       Have we rammed up our gates against the world.

*John and King Philip vow to fight to prove their claims to Angiers.
The Bastard mocks the armies and insults Austria. After the battle, the
French Herald announces the death of many English.*

1 Joker and patriot (in pairs)

The Bastard has remained quiet during the bombastic exchanges
between King John and King Philip. Now, he makes humorous asides
to the audience, and mixes together patriotism and bawdiness to insult
Austria.

Like King Henry V before Harfleur, the Bastard makes a patriotic
appeal to Saint George (line 288). But Shakespeare's audience would
have been reminded of an inn sign of the saint! Such inn signs of the
patron saint of England were common in Elizabethan times. However,
inn signs are another anachronism (see page 6), because they did not
exist in John's time.

The Bastard also makes sexual jokes at Austria's expense (lines
291–3). A 'lioness' was a prostitute, and 'ox-head' suggests that Austria's
wife has been unfaithful to him (because the horns of the ox signified
a cuckold). But in line 294, with the echo of Richard Cœur-de-lion,
the Bastard is sarcastic about Austria's call for 'peace'.

Rehearse ways of speaking the Bastard's lines, to bring out the
contrasts in his character.

2 How to stage the battle?

The stage direction '*excursions*' (between lines 299 and 300) describes
the comings and goings of battle. The director of every new production
of *King John* has to decide whether to stage the battle between the
English and French armies. What would you do? Advise a director
who has chosen to show the battle how it might be done, for example,
realistically, or symbolically (through the use of lighting and sound),
and so on.

---

witnesses John's army
else such-like
bloods brave soldiers
Stand in oppose
hold withhold
fleet die

swinged beat
some fence to sword-fight well
appointment order
**Speed then to take advantage of
the field** hurry to get the best
positions

KING JOHN Doth not the crown of England prove the king?
　　　　　And if not that, I bring you witnesses,
　　　　　Twice fifteen thousand hearts of England's breed –　　　275
BASTARD [*Aside*] Bastards and else.
KING JOHN To verify our title with their lives.
KING PHILIP As many and as well-born bloods as those –
BASTARD [*Aside*] Some bastards too.
KING PHILIP Stand in his face to contradict his claim.　　　280
CITIZEN Till you compound whose right is worthiest,
　　　　　We for the worthiest hold the right from both.
KING JOHN Then God forgive the sin of all those souls
　　　　　That to their everlasting residence,
　　　　　Before the dew of evening fall, shall fleet　　　285
　　　　　In dreadful trial of our kingdom's king!
KING PHILIP Amen, amen! Mount, chevaliers! To arms!
BASTARD Saint George that swinged the dragon, and e'er since
　　　　　Sits on his horseback at mine hostess' door,
　　　　　Teach us some fence! [*To Austria*] Sirrah, were I at home　　　290
　　　　　At your den, sirrah, with your lioness,
　　　　　I would set an ox-head to your lion's hide,
　　　　　To make a monster of you.
AUSTRIA　　　　　　　　　　　Peace, no more.
BASTARD O tremble, for you hear the lion roar.
KING JOHN Up higher to the plain, where we'll set forth　　　295
　　　　　In best appointment all our regiments.
BASTARD Speed then to take advantage of the field.
KING PHILIP It shall be so, and at the other hill
　　　　　Command the rest to stand. God and our right!
　　　　　　　　　　　　　　Exeunt. [*Citizens remain above*]

Here, after excursions, enter the HERALD OF FRANCE *with trumpets to the*
gates

FRENCH HERALD You men of Angiers, open wide your gates　　　300
　　　　　And let young Arthur Duke of Brittaine in,
　　　　　Who by the hand of France this day hath made
　　　　　Much work for tears in many an English mother,
　　　　　Whose sons lie scattered on the bleeding ground;
　　　　　Many a widow's husband grovelling lies　　　305
　　　　　Coldly embracing the discoloured earth,

The French Herald announces a French victory. The English Herald claims an English one. The Citizen judges that neither side has won. John again challenges King Philip.

1 A war of words: press release

Both the French and English Heralds use rhetoric to claim victory. Write a very brief press release, in not more than twelve words, for each. Your Chief of Propaganda has told you to express as much of the 'message' and tone of each Herald's words as possible. To help you, here's one way of understanding the English Herald's lines 312–23:

lines 312–14   Rejoice, King John the victor approaches

lines 315–16   Our soldiers are covered in French blood

lines 317–18   The feathers in our helmets are still there (For a medieval knight it was a disgrace to lose the plume of his crest (helmet) in battle.)

lines 319–20   We still have our battle flags ('colours')

lines 321–3   Like fox hunters, our soldiers' hands are covered with the blood of our enemy.

2 England 0 – France 0

Neither side has won. The Citizen's lines stress the balance and equality of the battle's outcome.

a The Citizen's verdict. Imagine your hands are a pair of scales. Read lines 325–33 'weighing' the contrasting or complementary words in each hand (for example, 'first/last', 'blood/blood').

b '*Enter the two kings with their powers.*' Suggest how the two stage armies might enter, to emphasise that the battle was a draw.

---

gilt gilded, covered
lusty eager
censurèd judged
several separate

passage course of a river
vexed angered, blocked
native normal
o'erswell overflow

And victory with little loss doth play
Upon the dancing banners of the French,
Who are at hand, triumphantly displayed,
To enter conquerors and to proclaim   310
Arthur of Brittaine England's king and yours.

Enter ENGLISH HERALD *with trumpet*

ENGLISH HERALD Rejoice, you men of Angiers, ring your bells;
King John, your king and England's, doth approach,
Commander of this hot malicious day.
Their armours, that marched hence so silver-bright,   315
Hither return all gilt with Frenchmen's blood,
There stuck no plume in any English crest
That is removèd by a staff of France;
Our colours do return in those same hands
That did display them when we first marched forth,   320
And like a jolly troop of huntsmen come
Our lusty English, all with purpled hands,
Dyed in the dying slaughter of their foes.
Open your gates and give the victors way.
CITIZEN Heralds, from off our tow'rs we might behold   325
From first to last the onset and retire
Of both your armies, whose equality
By our best eyes cannot be censurèd.
Blood hath bought blood, and blows have answered blows;
Strength matched with strength, and power confronted
power;   330
Both are alike, and both alike we like.
One must prove greatest. While they weigh so even,
We hold our town for neither, yet for both.

Enter the two kings with their powers, [ELEANOR, BLANCHE, *the*
BASTARD; *Lewis the* DAUPHIN, AUSTRIA] *at several doors*

KING JOHN France, hast thou yet more blood to cast away?
Say, shall the current of our right roam on,   335
Whose passage, vexed with thy impediment,
Shall leave his native channel and o'erswell
With course disturbed even thy confining shores,
Unless thou let his silver water keep
A peaceful progress to the ocean?   340

41

King Philip vows to fight to the death. The Bastard urges a return to battle. The Citizen refuses to admit either John or Philip. The Bastard compares the citizens of Angiers to a play audience.

1 Philip's vow (in pairs)

In lines 343–9, King Philip swears his support for Arthur.

a Compare this new-sworn oath with his vow in lines 41–3.
b Speak both oaths aloud. Is there a difference in tone?
c Do you think line 343 refers to Arthur or Philip?

2 A changed man? (in pairs)

The Bastard seems to use a different tone in lines 350–60. His joking, ironic style gives way to more serious, military language (see page 182). But does he really want to fight again, or is he just mocking King Philip's hyperbole (see page 186)? Speak the lines in two different ways: deadly serious, then mockingly and non-serious. Which seems the most appropriate?

3 An image of Death

The Bastard pictures Death as a person. Draw Death, using lines 352–5 as your inspiration ('chaps' = jaws, 'mousing' = tearing, biting).

4 'As in a theatre'

Shakespeare often emphasised the theatricality of the action he portrayed. In lines 373–6, the Bastard compares the citizens of Angiers to an audience at a play. If you were directing this scene, would you emphasise this comparison? If so, how would you tell the citizens to react?

---

hot trial battle
sways rules
climate sky
coupled joined
undetermined differences
 unresolved disputes
fronts faces

potents powers
confusion defeat
party side
own great deputy second only to
 God
former scruple previous doubts
Kinged ruled
scroyles scoundrels

KING PHILIP England, thou hast not saved one drop of blood
　　　　　　In this hot trial more than we of France,
　　　　　　Rather lost more. And by this hand I swear
　　　　　　That sways the earth this climate overlooks,
　　　　　　Before we will lay down our just-borne arms,　　　　345
　　　　　　We'll put thee down, 'gainst whom these arms we bear,
　　　　　　Or add a royal number to the dead,
　　　　　　Gracing the scroll that tells of this war's loss
　　　　　　With slaughter coupled to the name of kings.
BASTARD Ha, majesty! how high thy glory tow'rs,　　　　　　350
　　　　　　When the rich blood of kings is set on fire!
　　　　　　O now doth Death line his dead chaps with steel,
　　　　　　The swords of soldiers are his teeth, his fangs,
　　　　　　And now he feasts, mousing the flesh of men
　　　　　　In undetermined differences of kings.　　　　　　355
　　　　　　Why stand those royal fronts amazèd thus?
　　　　　　Cry 'havoc', kings! Back to the stainèd field,
　　　　　　You equal potents, fiery-kindled spirits.
　　　　　　Then let confusion of one part confirm
　　　　　　The other's peace. Till then, blows, blood, and death!　　360
KING JOHN Whose party do the townsmen yet admit?
KING PHILIP Speak, citizens, for England; who's your king?
CITIZEN The King of England, when we know the king.
KING PHILIP Know him in us that here hold up his right.
KING JOHN In us, that are our own great deputy　　　　　　365
　　　　　　And bear possession of our person here,
　　　　　　Lord of our presence, Angiers, and of you.
CITIZEN A greater pow'r than we denies all this,
　　　　　　And till it be undoubted, we do lock
　　　　　　Our former scruple in our strong-barred gates,　　　　370
　　　　　　Kinged of our fears, until our fears resolved
　　　　　　Be by some certain king, purged and deposed.
BASTARD By heaven, these scroyles of Angiers flout you, kings,
　　　　　　And stand securely on their battlements
　　　　　　As in a theatre, whence they gape and point　　　　375
　　　　　　At your industrious scenes and acts of death.
　　　　　　Your royal presences be ruled by me:

The Bastard proposes that England and France unite to destroy Angiers. Afterwards, they can continue to fight each other. King Philip and John readily agree.

King John, the Bastard and King Philip,
Royal Shakespeare Company, 1974.

1 'The policy' – political cunning (in pairs)

The Bastard proposes to make an 'unfencèd desolation' (universal destruction) of Angiers. The French and English armies should join forces ('conjointly bend') to attack, like the 'mutines of Jerusalem' (in 70 AD, warring factions inside Jerusalem temporarily united to fight the besieging Romans).

Imagine you are presenting a television news programme about the siege of Angiers. Work out exactly what the Bastard's plan entails. Present a clear report for your television audience.

soul-fearing terrifying	**minion** favourite
flinty ribs walls	**kiss** give
play aim guns, torment	**wild counsel** daring idea
jades worn out mares	**mighty states** powerful rulers
dissever your united strengths	**mettle** courage
separate again	**pell-mell** rush
cull choose	**stir** urge

Do like the mutines of Jerusalem,
Be friends awhile, and both conjointly bend
Your sharpest deeds of malice on this town.   380
By east and west let France and England mount
Their battering cannon chargèd to the mouths,
Till their soul-fearing clamours have brawled down
The flinty ribs of this contemptuous city.
I'd play incessantly upon these jades,   385
Even till unfencèd desolation
Leave them as naked as the vulgar air.
That done, dissever your united strengths
And part your mingled colours once again,
Turn face to face and bloody point to point;   390
Then in a moment Fortune shall cull forth
Out of one side her happy minion,
To whom in favour she shall give the day,
And kiss him with a glorious victory.
How like you this wild counsel, mighty states?   395
Smacks it not something of the policy?
KING JOHN Now by the sky that hangs above our heads,
I like it well. France, shall we knit our pow'rs,
And lay this Angiers even with the ground,
Then after fight who shall be king of it?   400
BASTARD And if thou hast the mettle of a king,
Being wronged as we are by this peevish town,
Turn thou the mouth of thy artillery,
As we will ours, against these saucy walls,
And when that we have dashed them to the ground,   405
Why then defy each other and pell-mell
Make work upon ourselves, for heaven or hell.
KING PHILIP Let it be so. Say, where will you assault?
KING JOHN We from the west will send destruction
Into this city's bosom.   410
AUSTRIA I from the north.
KING PHILIP   Our thunder from the south
Shall rain their drift of bullets on this town.
BASTARD [Aside] O prudent discipline! From north to south,
Austria and France shoot in each other's mouth.
I'll stir them to it. – Come, away, away!   415

45

The Citizen proposes that John and King Philip can both win without bloodshed, through the marriage of Lewis and Blanche. Nothing else will persuade the city to surrender.

1 The Citizen tries to persuade (in small groups)

The Citizen's argument follows a pattern:

lines 416–21 A suggestion for peace
lines 423–25 Blanche and Lewis are of the same age
lines 426–33 Blanche is a perfect match for Lewis
lines 434–40 They complement each other
lines 441–5 Their marriage would unite John and Philip
lines 446–50 Agreement will open the gates of Angiers
lines 450–5 Otherwise, Angiers will furiously defend itself.

The lines contain a proposal, reasons, compliments, balanced phrases, extended metaphor, threats and bombast (see page 186, Rhetoric).

Identify which lines reflect these characteristics of rhetoric (they may well overlap). Work out how the Citizen could use his tone of voice and actions to add to his powers of persuasion.

2 Blanche + Lewis = perfection

The Citizen argues a very complex 'proof' of how well Blanche (King John's niece) and Lewis (King Philip's son) complement each other (lines 434–40). Neither is complete without the other. Here's one way of presenting the Citizen's argument as a diagram. Invent your own image.

'fair divided excellence' + 'half part' = 'fullness of perfection'

Vouchsafe promise	**match of birth** marriage of people
fair-faced league a treaty that will	of equal rank
suit both sides	**complete of** perfect in
stroke sword stroke	**battery** bombardment
field battle	**swifter spleen** faster willingness
Persever continue	**mouth of passage** entrance gates
bent to hear willing to listen	**peremptory** determined

CITIZEN   Hear us, great kings. Vouchsafe awhile to stay,
          And I shall show you peace and fair-faced league.
          Win you this city without stroke or wound;
          Rescue those breathing lives to die in beds
          That here come sacrifices for the field.   420
          Persever not, but hear me, mighty kings.
KING JOHN   Speak on with favour, we are bent to hear.
CITIZEN   That daughter there of Spain, the Lady Blanche,
          Is niece to England. Look upon the years
          Of Lewis the Dauphin and that lovely maid.   425
          If lusty love should go in quest of beauty,
          Where should he find it fairer than in Blanche?
          If zealous love should go in search of virtue,
          Where should he find it purer than in Blanche?
          If love ambitious sought a match of birth,   430
          Whose veins bound richer blood than Lady Blanche?
          Such as she is, in beauty, virtue, birth,
          Is the young Dauphin every way complete.
          If not complete of, say he is not she,
          And she again wants nothing, to name want,   435
          If want it be not that she is not he.
          He is the half part of a blessèd man,
          Left to be finishèd by such as she,
          And she a fair divided excellence,
          Whose fullness of perfection lies in him.   440
          O, two such silver currents when they join
          Do glorify the banks that bound them in;
          And two such shores to two such streams made one,
          Two such controlling bounds shall you be, kings,
          To these two princes if you marry them.   445
          This union shall do more than battery can
          To our fast-closèd gates; for at this match,
          With swifter spleen than powder can enforce,
          The mouth of passage shall we fling wide ope
          And give you entrance. But without this match,   450
          The sea enragèd is not half so deaf,
          Lions more confident, mountains and rocks
          More free from motion – no, not Death himself
          In mortal fury half so peremptory
          As we to keep this city.

47

The Bastard mocks the Citizen's language. Stressing John's insecure right, Eleanor urges him to offer Blanche a large dowry. John offers all his French possessions except Angiers.

1 'The rotten carcass of old Death'

Compare the Bastard's lines 455–7 with the picture on the cover, and with lines 352–5.

2 Attacked with words (in pairs)

The Bastard makes fun of the Citizen's bombastic threats by asking the audience to laugh at the hyperbolic images used in lines 450–5. Speak the Bastard's lines 455–67, making them as humorous as possible. Remember that he is deliberately mocking the Citizen's rhetoric, so don't be afraid to 'go over the top'.

3 Accept! – Eleanor's reasons

Eleanor is very quick to urge King John to give a large dowry (marriage gift) to Blanche, to bring about the wedding ('knot') of Lewis and Blanche. She asks John to 'list to this conjunction' (listen to the proposed alliance), and reminds him that the marriage and dowry would cement more firmly his 'unsured assurance' (insecure right) to the English crown. She gives two reasons for accepting the marriage plan. First, in lines 472–3, she uses a metaphor of a fruit tree on which the sun does not shine, so preventing the green buds from blossoming and bearing fruit. Work out the second reason she gives, in lines 474–9.

4 The dowry

Turn to the map on page 3, to remind yourself of what King John is giving away in order to secure peace.

---

stay set-back
cannoneer soldier
bounce bang, noise
bastinado beating
buffets better hits harder
Zounds! God's wounds (a mild oath)

yielding likely agreement
capable of this ambition inclined to agree
Find liable to our crown consider subject to our rule
gild decorate
Holds hand with equals

BASTARD   Here's a stay   455
          That shakes the rotten carcass of old Death
          Out of his rags. Here's a large mouth indeed,
          That spits forth death and mountains, rocks and seas,
          Talks as familiarly of roaring lions
          As maids of thirteen do of puppy-dogs!   460
          What cannoneer begot this lusty blood?
          He speaks plain cannon-fire and smoke and bounce.
          He gives the bastinado with his tongue.
          Our ears are cudgelled, not a word of his
          But buffets better than a fist of France.   465
          Zounds! I was never so bethumped with words
          Since I first called my brother's father Dad.
          [KING PHILIP *and* LEWIS *move aside and whisper*]
ELEANOR Son, list to this conjunction, make this match,
          Give with our niece a dowry large enough,
          For by this knot thou shalt so surely tie   470
          Thy now unsured assurance to the crown
          That yon green boy shall have no sun to ripe
          The bloom that promiseth a mighty fruit.
          I see a yielding in the looks of France.
          Mark how they whisper. Urge them while their souls   475
          Are capable of this ambition,
          Lest zeal now melted by the windy breath
          Of soft petitions, pity, and remorse,
          Cool and congeal again to what it was.
CITIZEN Why answer not the double majesties   480
          This friendly treaty of our threatened town?
KING PHILIP Speak England first, that hath been forward first
          To speak unto this city: what say you?
KING JOHN If that the Dauphin there, thy princely son,
          Can in this book of beauty read, 'I love',   485
          Her dowry shall weigh equal with a queen,
          For Anjou and fair Touraine, Maine, Poitiers,
          And all that we upon this side the sea
          (Except this city now by us besieged)
          Find liable to our crown and dignity,   490
          Shall gild her bridal bed and make her rich
          In titles, honours, and promotions,
          As she in beauty, education, blood,
          Holds hand with any princess of the world.

Lewis declares his love for Blanche, in flowery phrases. The Bastard pokes fun at the treacherous imagery in Lewis's language. Blanche agrees to do what John wishes.

Lewis, King Philip, Blanche and King John. Choose a line from the script opposite as a suitable caption. (Blanche's lines 511–20 are spoken to Lewis.)

1 The language of love ? (in pairs)

Puns and artificial language fill Lewis's declaration of love.

a 'I never loved myself.' Look into your partner's eyes. What do you see? Work out three meanings of Lewis's use of 'shadow'.

b 'Love's traitor.' The Bastard continues to act as a commentator. He mocks Lewis's language, just as he mocked the Citizen's. In Shakespeare's day, the punishment for treason was to be 'hanged, drawn and quartered' (hung by the neck, cut down while still alive, disembowelled and cut into four). Talk together about what point you think the Bastard's mocking comparison is making.

---

shadow image
Drawn in pictured in
table artist's canvas (flat surface to paint on)
quartered lodged
translate it adjust it

will wish
properly precisely
churlish ungenerous
still always
vouchsafe choose

KING PHILIP What sayst thou, boy? Look in the lady's face.   495
LEWIS I do, my lord, and in her eye I find
      A wonder or a wondrous miracle,
      The shadow of myself formed in her eye,
      Which being but the shadow of your son,
      Becomes a sun and makes your son a shadow.   500
      I do protest I never loved myself
      Till now enfixèd I beheld myself
      Drawn in the flattering table of her eye.
               Whispers with Blanche
BASTARD [*Aside*] Drawn in the flattering table of her eye!
      Hanged in the frowning wrinkle of her brow!   505
      And quartered in her heart! he doth espy
        Himself love's traitor. This is pity now,
      That hanged and drawn and quartered there should be
      In such a love so vile a lout as he.
BLANCHE My uncle's will in this respect is mine.   510
      If he see aught in you that makes him like,
      That anything he sees which moves his liking,
      I can with ease translate it to my will;
      Or if you will, to speak more properly,
      I will enforce it eas'ly to my love.   515
      Further I will not flatter you, my lord,
      That all I see in you is worthy love,
      Than this: that nothing do I see in you –
      Though churlish thoughts themselves should be your
          judge –
      That I can find should merit any hate.   520
KING JOHN What say these young ones? What say you, my niece?
BLANCHE That she is bound in honour still to do
      What you in wisdom still vouchsafe to say.
KING JOHN Speak then, Prince Dauphin; can you love this lady?
LEWIS Nay, ask me if I can refrain from love,   525
      For I do love her most unfeignedly.

John offers a very generous dowry. The marriage is approved and will take place in Angiers. Philip worries about Constance's reaction. John awards Arthur two titles and Angiers.

1 'They join hands and kiss' (in pairs)

King Philip and Austria give Blanche and Lewis instructions (lines 533–5), which they obey. Write detailed notes for the actors playing Blanche and Lewis. Specify how you think they should perform the embrace, in order to show how they really feel about their forthcoming marriage. Alternatively, act out the stage directions with your partner.

2 Constance's feelings (in pairs)

a 'Sad and passionate'

Constance and Arthur left the stage at line 299. Constance was silenced at line 195, and has not spoken since. She does not yet know of King John's decision to give away so much of the Angevin Empire. But Lewis reports that she is 'sad and passionate' (line 544). Improvise a dialogue between Constance and her maid, to show how and why she feels this way.

b Two titles and Angiers

To appease Constance, John creates Arthur Duke of Brittany, Earl of Richmond and Lord of Angiers (lines 551–3). What do you think Constance's reaction to this gift will be? Check your guess as you read on.

---

pleased withal satisfied with this
close hold
assured (line 534) sure
assured (line 535) betrothed
amity friendship
presently immediately
league treaty/alliance
vantage advantage

repair / To our solemnity come to the wedding
fill up the measure of her will give all she wanted
stop her exclamation quieten her protests
suffer allow

KING JOHN Then do I give Volquessen, Touraine, Maine,
    Poitiers and Anjou, these five provinces
    With her to thee, and this addition more:
    Full thirty thousand marks of English coin. 530
    Philip of France, if thou be pleased withal,
    Command thy son and daughter to join hands.
KING PHILIP It likes us well. Young princes, close your hands.
AUSTRIA And your lips too, for I am well assured,
    That I did so when I was first assured. 535
               [They join hands and kiss]
KING PHILIP Now, citizens of Angiers, ope your gates,
    Let in that amity which you have made,
    For at Saint Mary's Chapel presently
    The rites of marriage shall be solemnised. –
    Is not the Lady Constance in this troop? 540
    I know she is not, for this match made up,
    Her presence would have interrupted much.
    Where is she and her son? Tell me, who knows.
LEWIS She is sad and passionate at your highness' tent.
KING PHILIP And by my faith, this league that we have made 545
    Will give her sadness very little cure.
    Brother of England, how may we content
    This widow lady? In her right we came,
    Which we, God knows, have turned another way,
    To our own vantage.
KING JOHN   We will heal up all, 550
    For we'll create young Arthur Duke of Brittaine
    And Earl of Richmond, and this rich fair town
    We make him lord of. Call the Lady Constance.
    With speedy messenger bid her repair
    To our solemnity. I trust we shall, 555
    If not fill up the measure of her will,
    Yet in some measure satisfy her so
    That we shall stop her exclamation.
    Go we as well as haste will suffer us
    To this unlooked-for, unprepared pomp. 560
               Exeunt [all but the Bastard]

The Bastard reflects on the fickleness of John and King Philip. He blames 'Commodity' (self-interest), which corrupts everything and everybody. He resolves to follow the kings' example.

1 Commodity: putting yourself first (in small groups)

The Bastard's soliloquy has six sections:

line 561	The world, kings and treaty are all mad
lines 562–6	John's cynical political move; Philip's integrity
lines 566–82	Commodity's crookedness affects everyone
lines 582–6	Commodity changes Philip's integrity to dishonour
lines 587–96	The reason for disliking Commodity: poverty!
lines 597–8	I'll follow my own self-interest!

a It's a mad, mad, mad world

Share out the soliloquy: each person reads up to a punctuation mark, then hands on. Next, share the lines as a friendly conversation, or as a logical argument.

b Look after number one

Commodity is personified in lines 566–82 as someone who has whispered ('rounded') in King Philip's ear, a changer of people's minds ('purpose-changer'), a 'sly devil', a 'broker' (go-between), who is plausible ('smooth-faced') and 'wins of all' (gets the better of). Imagine you wish to show 'Commodity' as a person. Suggest how the character would appear (dress, behaviour, and so on).

c Bowls

Lines 574–81 contain an extended image of the game of bowls. Because a bowl has a lead weight inserted, it cannot roll straight; its 'bias' makes it curve. Although the world is balanced ('peisèd'), Commodity makes it deviate ('This sway of motion'), losing all neutrality ('take head from all indifferency').

---

composition treaty
title in the whole claim to the whole lands
departed given up, left
pate skull, head
maids virgins
no external thing nothing

peisèd balanced
bawd pimp
Clapped on caught
rail scold
clutch close
angels gold coins (see page 80)
unattempted untempted

BASTARD Mad world, mad kings, mad composition!
John, to stop Arthur's title in the whole,
Hath willingly departed with a part,
And France, whose armour conscience buckled on,
Whom zeal and charity brought to the field   565
As God's own soldier, rounded in the ear
With that same purpose-changer, that sly devil,
That broker that still breaks the pate of faith,
That daily break-vow, he that wins of all,
Of kings, of beggars, old men, young men, maids –   570
Who having no external thing to lose
But the word 'maid', cheats the poor maid of that –
That smooth-faced gentleman, tickling Commodity,
Commodity, the bias of the world,
The world, who of itself is peisèd well,   575
Made to run even upon even ground,
Till this advantage, this vile-drawing bias,
This sway of motion, this Commodity,
Makes it take head from all indifferency,
From all direction, purpose, course, intent;   580
And this same bias, this Commodity,
This bawd, this broker, this all-changing word,
Clapped on the outward eye of fickle France,
Hath drawn him from his own-determined aid,
From a resolved and honourable war,   585
To a most base and vile-concluded peace.
And why rail I on this Commodity?
But for because he hath not wooed me yet.
Not that I have the power to clutch my hand
When his fair angels would salute my palm,   590
But for my hand, as unattempted yet,
Like a poor beggar raileth on the rich.
Well, whiles I am a beggar I will rail,
And say there is no sin but to be rich;
And being rich, my virtue then shall be   595
To say there is no vice but beggary.
Since kings break faith upon commodity,
Gain, be my lord, for I will worship thee.   *Exit*

Looking back at Act 2
Activities for groups or individuals

1 Policy: war and commodity

Act 2 is much concerned with war. It ends with the Bastard's lines on
'Commodity' (self-interest). Both war and Commodity are aspects of
'policy' (the use of power by a country or ruler). King John's and King
Philip's cynical disregard for the fate of the citizens of Angiers is a vivid
example of 'policy'.

a War on the stage. At line 333, the stage direction instructs:
'*Enter the two kings with their powers* (armies) *at several* (separate)
doors'. Write notes to suggest how the entry could be made to
display 'policy' in action.

b War in reality. Austria describes the campaign against Angiers
and England as 'a just and charitable war' (line 36). Talk together
about whether you think that war can ever be 'just and charitable'.

c 'Cry "havoc" kings!' (line 357). To cry 'havoc' was the chilling
signal for indiscriminate slaughter of everyone involved in battle.
Imagine that you are one of John's soldiers. Write a letter home,
describing your experience of all that has happened in Act 2.

'A bloody siege.' In Act 2, King John and King Philip talk of destroying
Angiers. But medieval sieges were long and difficult affairs. Stone-
throwing engines and mining under the walls were the two major methods
available to attackers of a fortified town. If the foundation was rock, mining
was impossible. Defenders could use cross-bows to great advantage.
Cylindrical walls made the attackers' task even more difficult.

2 A marriage of convenience?

The marriage of Lewis and Blanche marks the end of hostilities. In the past, the marriage of two important people to cement treaties or to prevent wars was a very important part of diplomacy. Arranged marriages still take place today. Take parts as a parent and a son or daughter. Improvise a dialogue in which the parent explains that a marriage has been arranged.

3 A change of policy

King Philip knows that Constance will not be pleased with his betrayal of her son's cause (lines 545–9). Imagine that you are the editor of a tabloid newspaper. Design a front page, to tell your readers all about the forthcoming royal marriage. Then write the story as it would be reported in a 'serious' newspaper.

Lion-hearted? In legend, the Bastard's father, Richard Cœur-de-lion, killed a lion that the Duke of Austria set on him (see page 20). Austria now wears a lion-skin as a sign of bravery!

Constance is appalled at the news of the marriage of Lewis and Blanche. She demands that Salisbury deny the story, but his actions and words confirm the truth.

1 A Messenger brings bad news (in pairs)

Salisbury has told Constance about the marriage of Lewis and Blanche, and about King John giving away much of his French territory. In lines 1–26, Constance expresses her dismay and anger at the news. Try some of the following to work out how Constance reacts to the news:

a Emphasise! Prod your partner with your finger as you speak each sentence.

b Implore! Quietly and sorrowfully beg Salisbury to deny his story.

c Ignore! Walk around the room, ignoring Salisbury. Speak the lines aloud to yourself, changing direction at each sentence. Salisbury must follow, trying to keep up, repeating one or two words from each sentence.

d Try it in the style of Cleopatra! In *Antony and Cleopatra*, the Messenger who brings Cleopatra the bad news that Antony is married, is beaten by Cleopatra. Try playing Constance in that style: take hold of your Messenger's arm and pull him or her around the room, changing direction at each line. Remember – safety first! Nobody must be in real danger.

e React! Work out how you think Salisbury should behave as Constance speaks her lines (you will find help at lines 19–23). Also, decide how Arthur should behave, as his mother harangues Salisbury.

Afterwards, talk together about how you think Constance should deliver the lines on stage (for example, does she vary her tone from line to line?).

---

a king's oath Philip's promise
capable of susceptible to, open to
take a truce be calm
that lamentable rheum those
  sorrowful tears

proud flooded
peering o'er his bounds
  overflowing its banks

ACT 3 SCENE 1
Outside the walls of Angiers

Enter (from the tent of the King of France) CONSTANCE,
ARTHUR *and* SALISBURY

CONSTANCE Gone to be married? Gone to swear a peace?
    False blood to false blood joined. Gone to be friends?
    Shall Lewis have Blanche and Blanche those provinces?
    It is not so; thou hast misspoke, misheard.
    Be well advised, tell o'er thy tale again.   5
    It cannot be, thou dost but say 'tis so.
    I trust I may not trust thee, for thy word
    Is but the vain breath of a common man.
    Believe me, I do not believe thee, man;
    I have a king's oath to the contrary.   10
    Thou shalt be punished for thus frighting me,
    For I am sick and capable of fears,
    Oppressed with wrongs and therefore full of fears,
    A widow, husbandless, subject to fears;
    A woman, naturally born to fears;   15
    And though thou now confess thou didst but jest,
    With my vexed spirits I cannot take a truce,
    But they will quake and tremble all this day.
    What dost thou mean by shaking of thy head?
    Why dost thou look so sadly on my son?   20
    What means that hand upon that breast of thine?
    Why holds thine eye that lamentable rheum,
    Like a proud river peering o'er his bounds?
    Be these sad signs confirmers of thy words?
    Then speak again, not all thy former tale,   25
    But this one word: whether thy tale be true.
SALISBURY As true as I believe you think them false
    That give you cause to prove my saying true.

Dismayed, Constance tries to dismiss Salisbury for bringing bad news. She tells Arthur that he deserves to inherit the crown because of his outstanding qualities, but fickle Fortune has cheated him.

Constance and Arthur. Shakespeare portrays Arthur as a young, vulnerable boy. In lines 51–61, Constance says that Nature has been generous to Arthur, endowing him with beauty comparable to that of the lily or the rose. But Fortune (the goddess of luck) does not smile on him. Instead, she behaves like a prostitute ('strumpet'), favouring King John and using King Philip of France as a pimp ('bawd') to defeat Arthur's rightful claims.

encounter battle	**half-blown** half-blossomed
brook endure, bear	**won from thee** abandons you
heinous wicked, odious	**Sh'adulterates hourly** she is
wert were	unfaithful to you often (or
swart swarthy	whore-ly: like a prostitute)
prodigious monstrous	**Envenom** poison
Become match, adorn	**underbear** endure, suffer

CONSTANCE O, if thou teach me to believe this sorrow,
     Teach thou this sorrow how to make me die,   30
     And let belief and life encounter so
     As doth the fury of two desperate men
     Which in the very meeting fall and die.
     Lewis marry Blanche! O boy, then where art thou?
     France friend with England! What becomes of me?   35
     Fellow, be gone: I cannot brook thy sight;
     This news hath made thee a most ugly man.
SALISBURY What other harm have I, good lady, done
     But spoke the harm that is by others done?
CONSTANCE Which harm within itself so heinous is   40
     As it makes harmful all that speak of it.
ARTHUR I do beseech you, madam, be content.
CONSTANCE If thou that bid'st me be content wert grim,
     Ugly, and sland'rous to thy mother's womb,
     Full of unpleasing blots and sightless stains,   45
     Lame, foolish, crooked, swart, prodigious,
     Patched with foul moles and eye-offending marks,
     I would not care, I then would be content,
     For then I should not love thee; no, nor thou
     Become thy great birth nor deserve a crown.   50
     But thou art fair, and at thy birth, dear boy,
     Nature and Fortune joined to make thee great.
     Of Nature's gifts thou mayst with lilies boast,
     And with the half-blown rose. But Fortune, O,
     She is corrupted, changed, and won from thee;   55
     Sh'adulterates hourly with thine uncle John,
     And with her golden hand hath plucked on France
     To tread down fair respect of sovereignty,
     And made his majesty the bawd to theirs.
     France is a bawd to Fortune and King John –   60
     That strumpet Fortune, that usurping John.
     Tell me, thou fellow, is not France forsworn?
     Envenom him with words, to get thee gone
     And leave those woes alone which I alone
     Am bound to underbear.
SALISBURY   Pardon me, madam,   65
     I may not go without you to the kings.

Constance sits down in sorrow, refusing to go to the kings. King Philip declares the marriage day an eternal festival, but Constance calls it a day of shame and disasters.

1 Grief

Constance uses personification in line 69, 'For Grief is proud and makes his owner stoop'. Close your eyes and conjure up the picture which Constance's image of Grief evokes in your mind. Talk together with other students about whether they 'see' similar images to your own.

2 What's true?

King Philip enters, saying to his new daughter-in-law, Blanche, "Tis true'. But what's true? Invent two lines for Blanche to speak that would lead naturally to Philip's line 75.

3 Red-letter day – or unlucky day?

King Philip declares the marriage day a festival day of perpetual sunshine. Such festival days (for example, Christmas Day and Good Friday) were marked in gold or red ('golden letters', line 85) on Elizabethan calendars. This was the origin of the saying 'a red-letter day', meaning a happy, important occasion.

Constance says the wedding day is shameful and unlucky. On its anniversary, children will be born deformed, ships wrecked and contracts broken. She sees it as a wicked day, not a 'holy day' (holiday).

Identify each time the word 'day' is used in lines 75–97. Decide how you think the word should be spoken on each occasion.

---

state condition (or throne)
Stays in his course stands still
plays the alchemist turns all
  to gold
meagre barren
high tides festival times

perjury breaking oaths
burthens babies
prodigiously be crossed are born
  as monsters
But on except for
pawned pledged, promised

CONSTANCE Thou mayst, thou shalt, I will not go with thee;
    I will instruct my sorrows to be proud,
    For Grief is proud and makes his owner stoop.
    To me and to the state of my great grief   70
    Let kings assemble, for my grief's so great
    That no supporter but the huge firm earth
    Can hold it up.
       [Sits on the ground]
       Here I and sorrows sit,
    Here is my throne, bid kings come bow to it.
             [Exit Salisbury]

Enter KING JOHN, *[hand in hand with* KING PHILIP *of]* France, *[Lewis
the]* DAUPHIN, BLANCHE, ELEANOR, *Philip [the* BASTARD], AUSTRIA,
[and attendants]

KING PHILIP 'Tis true, fair daughter, and this blessèd day 75
    Ever in France shall be kept festival.
    To solemnise this day the glorious sun
    Stays in his course and plays the alchemist,
    Turning with splendour of his precious eye
    The meagre cloddy earth to glittering gold.   80
    The yearly course that brings this day about
    Shall never see it but a holiday.
CONSTANCE A wicked day, and not a holy day. *[Rises]*
    What hath this day deserved? what hath it done
    That it in golden letters should be set   85
    Among the high tides in the calendar?
    Nay, rather turn this day out of the week,
    This day of shame, oppression, perjury.
    Or if it must stand still, let wives with child
    Pray that their burthens may not fall this day, 90
    Lest that their hopes prodigiously be crossed.
    But on this day let seamen fear no wreck,
    No bargains break that are not this day made;
    This day all things begun, come to ill end,
    Yea, faith itself to hollow falsehood change. 95
KING PHILIP By heaven, lady, you shall have no cause
    To curse the fair proceedings of this day.
    Have I not pawned to you my majesty?

Constance accuses King Philip of betraying her trust. She calls on God to make war between France and England, and charges Austria with cowardice. The Bastard echoes her taunt of cowardice.

1 No true king

Constance complains she has been 'beguiled' (deceived) with a 'counterfeit' (false coin) which, being 'touched and tried' (tested for purity), proves valueless (lines 99–101). For her, King Philip is no true king, he only resembles majesty. In Shakespeare's time, coins were 'touched' on a touchstone, to discover if they were pure gold or not.

Sketch two coins to match Constance's image. One shows Philip as a true king, the other as a false king.

2 Taunting Austria (in pairs)

Austria urges peace; Constance accuses him of cowardice. To emphasise her contempt, she often addresses him as 'thou', which could, in some circumstances, be used to an inferior. One person reads aloud lines 113–29. The other echoes (scornfully) every 'thou', 'thee' or 'thy'. Then change over. This time, the partner echoes every word likely to be spoken contemptuously (for example, 'shame', 'slave', 'wretch' and 'coward'). You will find that even words which seem complimentary can be spoken disdainfully and dismissively. For greater emphasis, prod Austria with your finger each time you speak a word scornfully.

3 The Bastard joins in

The Bastard joins in the taunting of Austria. He repeats Constance's 'And hang a calf's-skin on those recreant limbs'. Work out how the Bastard could deliver the line for greatest audience enjoyment.

---

forsworn perjured, promise-breakers
amity friendship
perjured forsworn, oath-breaking
spoil war booty (Cœur-de-lion's lion-skin)
Fortune's champion backer only of winning sides

humorous changeable, fickle
sooth'st up greatness
  flatters important people
ramping over-acting, roaring
party side, cause
fall over desert, join
Doff it take it off
recreant cowardly

CONSTANCE You have beguiled me with a counterfeit
              Resembling majesty, which being touched and tried,   100
              Proves valueless. You are forsworn, forsworn.
              You came in arms to spill enemies' blood,
              But now in arms you strengthen it with yours.
              The grappling vigour and rough frown of war
              Is cold in amity and painted peace,   105
              And our oppression hath made up this league.
              Arm, arm, you heavens, against these perjured kings!
              A widow cries; be husband to me, God!
              Let not the hours of this ungodly day
              Wear out the day in peace; but ere sun set,   110
              Set armèd discord 'twixt these perjured kings!
              Hear me, O, hear me!
AUSTRIA   Lady Constance, peace.
CONSTANCE War, war, no peace! Peace is to me a war.
              O Limoges, O Austria, thou dost shame
              That bloody spoil. Thou slave, thou wretch, thou coward!   115
              Thou little valiant, great in villainy!
              Thou ever strong upon the stronger side!
              Thou Fortune's champion that dost never fight
              But when her humorous ladyship is by
              To teach thee safety! Thou art perjured too,   120
              And sooth'st up greatness. What a fool art thou,
              A ramping fool, to brag and stamp and swear
              Upon my party. Thou cold-blooded slave,
              Hast thou not spoke like thunder on my side,
              Been sworn my soldier, bidding me depend   125
              Upon thy stars, thy fortune, and thy strength,
              And dost thou now fall over to my foes?
              Thou wear a lion's hide! Doff it for shame,
              And hang a calf's-skin on those recreant limbs.
AUSTRIA O that a man should speak those words to me!   130
BASTARD And hang a calf's-skin on those recreant limbs.
AUSTRIA Thou dar'st not say so, villain, for thy life.
BASTARD And hang a calf's-skin on those recreant limbs.
KING JOHN We like not this, thou dost forget thyself.

Pandulph demands to know why John rejects Stephen Langton as Archbishop of Canterbury. John ridicules the Pope, saying he alone, as king, rules in England. He condemns all those who support the Pope.

1 Insults all round

King John insults Pandulph and the Pope (lines 147–60). He then insults King Philip for fearing the Pope (lines 162–71). Experiment with ways of speaking John's lines, to bring out the contempt and sarcasm of his words.

Pandulph, Royal Shakespeare Company, 1974. Pope Innocent III tried to appoint Stephen Langton as Archbishop of Canterbury in 1207. King John resisted the appointment for seven years, and was excommunicated as a result (see pages 68 and 176). John finally submitted, and Langton was made Archbishop in 1214.

legate ambassador, emissary
spurn reject
force perforce by force
see bishopric (bishop's territory), diocese
earthy name to interrogatories merely human questioner
task demand, force
tithe or toll collect taxes

all reverence set apart without respect
grossly stupidly
vild vile
dross scum, waste matter
pardon (see page 96)
This juggling ... cherish reward false belief with money

Enter PANDULPH

KING PHILIP Here comes the holy legate of the Pope.   135
PANDULPH Hail, you anointed deputies of God!
　　　　To thee, King John, my holy errand is.
　　　　I Pandulph, of fair Milan cardinal,
　　　　And from Pope Innocent the legate here,
　　　　Do in his name religiously demand   140
　　　　Why thou against the church, our holy mother,
　　　　So wilfully dost spurn, and force perforce
　　　　Keep Stephen Langton, chosen Archbishop
　　　　Of Canterbury, from that holy see.
　　　　This, in our foresaid Holy Father's name,   145
　　　　Pope Innocent, I do demand of thee.
KING JOHN What earthy name to interrogatories
　　　　Can task the free breath of a sacred king?
　　　　Thou canst not, cardinal, devise a name
　　　　So slight, unworthy, and ridiculous   150
　　　　To charge me to an answer, as the Pope.
　　　　Tell him this tale, and from the mouth of England
　　　　Add thus much more: that no Italian priest
　　　　Shall tithe or toll in our dominions,
　　　　But as we under God are supreme head,   155
　　　　So under Him, that great supremacy
　　　　Where we do reign, we will alone uphold
　　　　Without th'assistance of a mortal hand.
　　　　So tell the Pope, all reverence set apart
　　　　To him and his usurped authority.   160
KING PHILIP Brother of England, you blaspheme in this.
KING JOHN Though you and all the kings of Christendom
　　　　Are led so grossly by this meddling priest,
　　　　Dreading the curse that money may buy out,
　　　　And by the merit of vild gold, dross, dust,   165
　　　　Purchase corrupted pardon of a man,
　　　　Who in that sale sells pardon from himself –
　　　　Though you and all the rest so grossly led,
　　　　This juggling witchcraft with revenue cherish,
　　　　Yet I alone, alone do me oppose   170
　　　　Against the Pope and count his friends my foes.

Pandulph excommunicates John and calls for his assassination. Constance claims all law under John is corrupt. Pandulph, Austria and Lewis appeal to King Philip to break with John. The Bastard mocks Austria.

1 Excommunication – and assassination (in pairs)

In the time of King John, excommunication was a terrible threat for Christians. It removed offenders from all contact with the Church, so that they ran the risk of eternal damnation. Pandulph adds an extra dimension to his condemnation of John: any person who assassinates John, by any means, will be made a saint (lines 176–9).

Queen Elizabeth I was similarly excommunicated by the Roman Catholic Church, which likewise called for her assassination. In 1583, when Shakespeare was nineteen, his cousin Edward Arden was executed for conspiring to kill Elizabeth. The dangers of excommunication and assassination were therefore present in Shakespeare's mind, as they were in the minds of his fellow citizens in Elizabethan England.

Talk together about whether you think excommunication is something which creates fear in people's minds today. Also discuss what you think about people of a particular faith or country being urged to murder others in the name of religion.

2 Law

Is the law always impartial and 'right'? Constance does not think so, and complains strongly in lines 185–90 that, because John is king, the law that comes from his authority is unjust. Decide:

a What (or whose) 'law' does Pandulph have in mind in line 184? Is it the same 'law' that Constance refers to in the following lines?

b Do you think 'law' can be impartial, or will it always be biased to serve the interests of those in authority, who make the law?

---

heretic opponent of a religious belief
Canonised created a saint
warrant justification
bar exclude

raise the power use the armies
disjoining releasing
pocket up these wrongs endure these slanders
Bethink think carefully

PANDULPH Then by the lawful power that I have
          Thou shalt stand cursed and excommunicate,
          And blessèd shall he be that doth revolt
          From his allegiance to an heretic,   175
          And meritorious shall that hand be called,
          Canonised and worshipped as a saint,
          That takes away by any secret course
          Thy hateful life.
CONSTANCE   O lawful let it be
          That I have room with Rome to curse a while!   180
          Good father cardinal, cry thou 'Amen'
          To my keen curses; for without my wrong
          There is no tongue hath power to curse him right.
PANDULPH There's law and warrant, lady, for my curse.
CONSTANCE And for mine too, when law can do no right,   185
          Let it be lawful that law bar no wrong.
          Law cannot give my child his kingdom here,
          For he that holds his kingdom holds the law.
          Therefore, since law itself is perfect wrong,
          How can the law forbid my tongue to curse?   190
PANDULPH Philip of France, on peril of a curse,
          Let go the hand of that arch-heretic,
          And raise the power of France upon his head,
          Unless he do submit himself to Rome.
ELEANOR Look'st thou pale, France? Do not let go thy hand.   195
CONSTANCE [*To King John*] Look to it, devil, lest that France
              repent
          And by disjoining hands hell lose a soul.
AUSTRIA King Philip, listen to the cardinal.
BASTARD And hang a calf's-skin on his recreant limbs.
AUSTRIA Well ruffian, I must pocket up these wrongs,   200
          Because –
BASTARD   Your breeches best may carry them.
KING JOHN Philip, what say'st thou to the cardinal?
CONSTANCE What should he say, but as the cardinal?
LEWIS Bethink you, father, for the difference
          Is purchase of a heavy curse from Rome,   205
          Or the light loss of England for a friend:
          Forgo the easier.
BLANCHE   That's the curse of Rome.

Constance urges King Philip to keep his promise and support her cause. Pandulph reminds Philip of the threat of excommunication. Philip recalls his newly-sworn friendship with John after the recent battle.

'I am perplexed and know not what to say.' King Philip asks Pandulph to empathise with him ('make my person yours'), and say what he would do ('how you would bestow yourself') if he had Philip's dilemma.

1 Logic chopping (in pairs)

Just as Constance played with the word 'law' (lines 185–90), she now plays with 'need' and 'faith'. One person reads lines 211–16 a line at a time, pausing at the end of each line. In the pause, the other explains the line ('need' = my cause, the recognition of Arthur as the rightful king; 'faith' = your promise of friendship to King John).

---

untrimmèd undressed, unadorned
infer imply, show
bestow behave, decide
Married in league joined in alliance
but new before only newly-made
clap seal

pencil paint-brush
incensèd enraged
purged cleansed
Unyoke undo, release
kind regreet return of greeting and friendship

CONSTANCE O Lewis, stand fast! The devil tempts thee here
    In likeness of a new untrimmèd bride.
BLANCHE The Lady Constance speaks not from her faith,   210
    But from her need.
CONSTANCE   O, if thou grant my need,
    Which only lives but by the death of faith,
    That need must needs infer this principle,
    That faith would live again by death of need.
    O then tread down my need, and faith mounts up;   215
    Keep my need up, and faith is trodden down.
KING JOHN The king is moved and answers not to this.
CONSTANCE O, be removed from him and answer well!
AUSTRIA Do so, King Philip, hang no more in doubt.
BASTARD Hang nothing but a calf's-skin, most sweet lout.   220
KING PHILIP I am perplexed and know not what to say.
PANDULPH What canst thou say but will perplex thee more
    If thou stand excommunicate and cursed?
KING PHILIP Good reverend father, make my person yours,
    And tell me how you would bestow yourself.   225
    This royal hand and mine are newly knit,
    And the conjunction of our inward souls
    Married in league, coupled and linked together
    With all religious strength of sacred vows;
    The latest breath that gave the sound of words   230
    Was deep-sworn faith, peace, amity, true love
    Between our kingdoms and our royal selves.
    And even before this truce, but new before,
    No longer than we well could wash our hands
    To clap this royal bargain up of peace,   235
    God knows, they were besmeared and overstained
    With slaughter's pencil, where revenge did paint
    The fearful difference of incensèd kings.
    And shall these hands so lately purged of blood,
    So newly joined in love, so strong in both,   240
    Unyoke this seizure and this kind regreet?
    Play fast and loose with faith? so jest with heaven?

King Philip continues to protest that he cannot break his newly-made friendship with John. But Pandulph is utterly unyielding: Philip's duty to the Church demands that he must break with John.

1 Pandulph will not be moved

King Philip's lines 224–52 are a long plea for understanding. How can he break his promise of peace with King John, so soon after vowing friendship following a bloody battle? He begs Pandulph to revoke his demand and make 'Some gentle order' to enable peace to continue. But Pandulph seizes on 'order' and turns it on its head (line 253). Only war with England is acceptable.

Imagine that the actor playing Pandulph says to you, 'How can I show in lines 253–61 that I'm implacable?'. Advise him.

2 OK to break a promise?

Pandulph embarks on a long and tortuous argument to persuade King Philip to break his promise to King John. For many Protestants in Shakespeare's audience, Pandulph was the stereotype of the devious Catholic priest, putting forward complicated arguments to support a dubious cause.

But it is important to consider more than one view of Pandulph's argument. Try both of the following activities, to help you make up your mind about Pandulph (sincere or deceitful, logical or false):

a Experience the casuistry (the twisting and turning of the argument). Read lines 263–97 aloud as you walk around the room, changing direction at every punctuation mark. Alternatively, stay seated, but use your hands to show the changes in direction.

b Express the argument. Read the lines to each other slowly, a sentence at a time. Make your reading as sincere and as logical as possible, building up your argument point by point. You will find help with Pandulph's lines on page 74.

---

unconstant changeable
bloody host savage army
chafèd angry, wounded
mortal deadly
fasting hungry

faith/faith promise to John/ religious faith
amiss wrongly
purposes mistook taking a wrong direction

Make such unconstant children of ourselves
As now again to snatch our palm from palm,
Unswear faith sworn, and on the marriage-bed   245
Of smiling peace to march a bloody host,
And make a riot on the gentle brow
Of true sincerity? O holy sir,
My reverend father, let it not be so.
Out of your grace devise, ordain, impose   250
Some gentle order, and then we shall be blest
To do your pleasure and continue friends.

PANDULPH   All form is formless, order orderless,
Save what is opposite to England's love.
Therefore to arms! Be champion of our church,   255
Or let the church our mother breathe her curse,
A mother's curse, on her revolting son.
France, thou mayst hold a serpent by the tongue,
A chafèd lion by the mortal paw,
A fasting tiger safer by the tooth,   260
Than keep in peace that hand which thou dost hold.

KING PHILIP   I may disjoin my hand, but not my faith.

PANDULPH   So mak'st thou faith an enemy to faith,
And like a civil war sett'st oath to oath,
Thy tongue against thy tongue. O, let thy vow   265
First made to heaven, first be to heaven performed,
That is, to be the champion of our church.
What since thou swor'st, is sworn against thyself,
And may not be performèd by thyself,
For that which thou hast sworn to do amiss,   270
Is not amiss when it is truly done,
And being not done, where doing tends to ill,
The truth is then most done not doing it.
The better act of purposes mistook
Is to mistake again; though indirect,   275
Yet indirection thereby grows direct,
And falsehood falsehood cures, as fire cools fire
Within the scorchèd veins of one new burned.

Pandulph completes his tortuous argument, urging King Philip to break with John. Austria and Lewis support Pandulph. Blanche begs for peace, Constance for war.

1 Pandulph's argument (in pairs)

Pandulph develops his complex argument by playing with three major elements: King Philip's duty to God; Philip's promise of friendship with King John; the idea that bad promises should be broken. Read through Pandulph's argument using the following sections to help you:

lines 263–5	Your religious faith battles against your promise to John
lines 265–7	Honour your religious vows
lines 268–73	Your promise to John is wrong, so there's nothing wrong in breaking it
lines 274–8	Wrongdoing (breaking a promise) is the cure for wrongdoing
lines 279–83	Only religion is valid, and your promise to John is against religion
lines 283–285	You are unsure in your religious vows, but only religious vows are true
lines 286–7	Breaking your promise to John is to keep your faith with God
lines 288–94	Your promise to John betrays yourself, so it's noble to break it
lines 294–7	If you don't break with John, you will be cursed.

a Is Pandulph right? Is it right to break a promise? Can you think of examples from your own experience, where someone has broken a promise for what you think is a good reason?

b Philip is silent. He does not reply to Pandulph's long argument, even though it has all been addressed to him. But how does he react as Pandulph speaks? Advise him.

---

surety guarantee
giddy loose suggestions foolish
 temptations (your promise to John)
vouchsafe grant, allow
churlish rough, vulgar

measures of our pomp music at
 our wedding celebrations
doom forethought fate
 determined

It is religion that doth make vows kept,
But thou hast sworn against religion   280
By what thou swear'st against the thing thou swear'st,
And mak'st an oath the surety for thy truth
Against an oath. The truth thou art unsure
To swear swears only not to be forsworn –
Else what a mockery should it be to swear!   285
But thou dost swear only to be forsworn
And most forsworn, to keep what thou dost swear;
Therefore thy later vows, against thy first,
Is in thyself rebellion to thyself,
And better conquest never canst thou make   290
Than arm thy constant and thy nobler parts
Against these giddy loose suggestions;
Upon which better part our prayers come in,
If thou vouchsafe them. But if not, then know
The peril of our curses light on thee   295
So heavy as thou shalt not shake them off
But in despair die under their black weight.

AUSTRIA Rebellion, flat rebellion!

BASTARD   Will't not be?
    Will not a calf's-skin stop that mouth of thine?

LEWIS Father, to arms!

BLANCHE   Upon thy wedding-day?   300
    Against the blood that thou hast marrièd?
    What, shall our feast be kept with slaughtered men?
    Shall braying trumpets and loud churlish drums,
    Clamours of hell, be measures of our pomp?
    O husband, hear me. Aye, alack, how new   305
    Is 'husband' in my mouth! Even for that name
    Which till this time my tongue did ne'er pronounce,
    Upon my knee I beg, go not to arms
    Against mine uncle.

CONSTANCE O, upon my knee made hard with kneeling   310
    I do pray to thee, thou virtuous Dauphin,
    Alter not the doom forethought by heaven.

King Philip breaks with John. Constance rejoices, but Blanche feels torn by her loyalties to her husband and to her blood relations. John and Philip threaten each other and prepare for battle.

1 Dramatic effect (in pairs)

a 'Honour … honour … honour.' Advise Constance how to speak line 316 (for example, ironically, sincerely, or in some other way. Should she speak each 'honour' with different emphasis?).

b '*Drops King John's hand.*' On stage, King Philip's line 320 and his releasing of John's hand is always a moment of high drama. Work out how you would stage it for maximum dramatic effect.

2 Blanche's dilemma (in small groups)

Blanche expresses the cruel dilemma of a person caught up in a civil war or family feud. She owes loyalty to her husband and father-in-law (Lewis and King Philip), and to her uncle and grandmother (King John and Eleanor). Where does her allegiance lie? Talk together about what you would do in a similar dilemma.

3 Blanche and Lewis

Lewis ignores Blanche's plea at lines 313–14. In line 337, he orders her to throw in her lot with France. Blanche joins him, speaking line 338. What audience response would you wish to evoke at line 338? How might you achieve it?

4 'Old Time' – personification

In lines 324–5, the Bastard seems to say that Time will determine what happens in the coming battle. He personifies Time as a sexton (a church official who sets the clocks and digs the graves; see page 182).

I muse I wonder	**Assurèd loss** certain loser
profound respects strong arguments	**puissance** powers, army, forces
rue regret	**allay** relieve
dismember me tear me apart	**jeopardy** danger, peril
	let's hie let's hurry

BLANCHE   Now shall I see thy love. What motive may
　　　　　Be stronger with thee than the name of wife?
CONSTANCE   That which upholdeth him that thee upholds,　　　315
　　　　　His honour – O thine honour, Lewis, thine honour.
LEWIS   I muse your majesty doth seem so cold,
　　　　　When such profound respects do pull you on.
PANDULPH   I will denounce a curse upon his head.
KING PHILIP   Thou shalt not need. England, I will fall from thee.　　　320
　　　　　[Drops King John's hand]
CONSTANCE   O fair return of banished majesty.
ELEANOR   O foul revolt of French inconstancy.
KING JOHN   France, thou shalt rue this hour within this hour.
BASTARD   Old Time the clock-setter, that bald sexton Time,
　　　　　Is it as he will? Well then, France shall rue.　　　325
BLANCHE   The sun's o'ercast with blood. Fair day, adieu.
　　　　　Which is the side that I must go withal?
　　　　　I am with both, each army hath a hand,
　　　　　And in their rage, I having hold of both,
　　　　　They whirl asunder and dismember me.　　　330
　　　　　Husband, I cannot pray that thou mayst win;
　　　　　Uncle, I needs must pray that thou mayst lose.
　　　　　Father, I may not wish the fortune thine;
　　　　　Grandam, I will not wish thy wishes thrive.
　　　　　Whoever wins, on that side shall I lose,　　　335
　　　　　Assurèd loss, before the match be played.
LEWIS   Lady, with me, with me thy fortune lies.
BLANCHE   There where my fortune lives, there my life dies.
KING JOHN   Cousin, go draw our puissance together.
　　　　　　　　　　　　　　　　　[Exit Bastard]
　　　　　France, I am burned up with inflaming wrath,　　　340
　　　　　A rage whose heat hath this condition
　　　　　That nothing can allay, nothing but blood,
　　　　　The blood and dearest-valued blood of France.
KING PHILIP   Thy rage shall burn thee up, and thou shalt turn
　　　　　To ashes, ere our blood shall quench that fire.　　　345
　　　　　Look to thyself, thou art in jeopardy.
KING JOHN   No more than he that threats. – To arms let's hie!
　　　　　　　　　　　　　　　　Exeunt [severally]

A battle takes place between the armies of France and England. The Bastard has killed Austria and rescued Eleanor. Arthur, captured, is put into Hubert's keeping. John promises to be kind to Arthur.

'Alarums, excursions' (sound of drums and trumpets, and battles on stage). This is how a production of 1899 presented the battle.

1 Stage the battle

Work out how you would stage the different aspects of the battle in Scenes 2 and 3 opposite. Many modern productions omit all reference to Austria's head, because it makes the audience laugh.

2 Did Shakespeare forget?

In lines 4 and 5, the Bastard is called Philip, even though King John had earlier re-christened him Richard. Give reasons why you would, or would not, alter the name in performance.

---

breathes rests
make up advance
assailèd attacked
ta'en captured (taken)

liege lord
retreat trumpet call to order withdrawal

ACT 3   SCENE 2
A battlefield near Angiers

Alarums, excursions. Enter BASTARD *with Austria's head
and the lion's skin*

BASTARD   Now by my life, this day grows wondrous hot;
　　　　　Some airy devil hovers in the sky
　　　　　And pours down mischief. Austria's head lie there,
　　　　　While Philip breathes.

Enter KING JOHN, ARTHUR, HUBERT

KING JOHN   Hubert, keep this boy. Philip, make up:　　　　　5
　　　　　My mother is assailèd in our tent,
　　　　　And ta'en I fear.
BASTARD　　　　　　　My lord, I rescued her,
　　　　　Her highness is in safety, fear you not.
　　　　　But on, my liege, for very little pains
　　　　　Will bring this labour to an happy end.　　　　　10

Exeunt

ACT 3   SCENE 3
Another part of the battlefield

Alarums, excursions, retreat. Enter KING JOHN, ELEANOR,
ARTHUR, BASTARD, HUBERT, *lords*

KING JOHN   [*To Eleanor*] So shall it be; your grace shall stay behind
　　　　　So strongly guarded. [*To Arthur*] Cousin, look not sad,
　　　　　Thy grandam loves thee, and thy uncle will
　　　　　As dear be to thee as thy father was.
ARTHUR   O, this will make my mother die with grief!　　　　　5

John orders the Bastard to ransack the English churches for money to pay for the war. John thanks Hubert for his loyalty, promises future rewards, and hints that he has other things to say to Hubert.

'Imprisoned angels/Set at liberty.' King John orders the Bastard to spare no efforts in squeezing money out of the Church to fill his empty coffers. 'Angels' (line 8) is a pun and an anachronism, as such coins were not minted until the fifteenth century. They were gold coins with a picture of the Archangel Michael on one side. The Bastard accepts his plundering mission with alacrity. Not even the threat of excommunication will stop him ('Bell, book, and candle' were used in the ceremony of excommunication).

1 Is Eleanor involved in the plot?

King John is about to plot the murder of Arthur. He has sent the Bastard to England. So it seems that the Bastard is free of any involvement in John's murderous scheme. But is Eleanor party to John's plot? The stage direction at line 18 shows that she takes Arthur aside, to enable John to begin to work on Hubert. Talk together about whether you think Eleanor knows about John's intentions. Suggest how she should behave with Arthur during lines 19–69, so that the audience can share your view of Eleanor's innocence or complicity.

Cousin/Coz kinsman	**voluntary oath** freely-given pledge of loyalty
bags money-bags	
the hungry my soldiers	**bounden** indebted
commission authority	**wanton** merry
becks beckons	**gauds** worthless toys, showy trinkets
wall of flesh body	
advantage interest	

KING JOHN [*To Bastard*] Cousin, away for England, haste before,
    And ere our coming see thou shake the bags
    Of hoarding abbots; imprisoned angels
    Set at liberty. The fat ribs of peace
    Must by the hungry now be fed upon.   10
    Use our commission in his utmost force.
BASTARD Bell, book, and candle shall not drive me back,
    When gold and silver becks me to come on.
    I leave your highness. Grandam, I will pray,
    If ever I remember to be holy,   15
    For your fair safety. So I kiss your hand.
ELEANOR Farewell, gentle cousin.
KING JOHN   Coz, farewell.
                             [*Exit Bastard*]
ELEANOR Come hither, little kinsman; hark, a word.
              [*She takes Arthur aside*]
KING JOHN Come hither, Hubert. O, my gentle Hubert,
    We owe thee much. Within this wall of flesh   20
    There is a soul counts thee her creditor,
    And with advantage means to pay thy love,
    And, my good friend, thy voluntary oath
    Lives in this bosom, dearly cherishèd.
    Give me thy hand. I had a thing to say,   25
    But I will fit it with some better time.
    By heaven, Hubert, I am almost ashamed
    To say what good respect I have of thee.
HUBERT I am much bounden to your majesty.
KING JOHN Good friend, thou hast no cause to say so yet,   30
    But thou shalt have, and creep time ne'er so slow,
    Yet it shall come for me to do thee good.
    I had a thing to say, but let it go.
    The sun is in the heaven, and the proud day,
    Attended with the pleasures of the world,   35
    Is all too wanton, and too full of gauds
    To give me audience. If the midnight bell
    Did with his iron tongue and brazen mouth
    Sound on into the drowsy ear of night,
    If this same were a churchyard where we stand,   40
    And thou possessèd with a thousand wrongs;

John continues his devious plotting. Hubert promises total obedience, and John promptly orders Arthur's death. Leaving Eleanor in Angiers, John and the others depart for Calais and England.

1 Employing a murderer: hesitation and evasion
(in pairs)

King John says twice, 'I had a thing to say', but he takes a long time to make his intention perfectly clear to Hubert. The following activities will help you understand how John goes about his task:

a Flattering Hubert (lines 19–32). One person speaks the lines, the other echoes every word that praises Hubert and promises him reward.

b If only ... (lines 34–53)! John says that sunshine and daylight are not a suitable backdrop for what he has to say (lines 34–7). If only it were midnight in a churchyard (lines 37–40); if only Hubert were villainous or melancholy (lines 41–7); if only Hubert could understand, without John having to speak (lines 48–51). If any of these things were so, then John would speak freely (lines 52–3). One person reads lines 34–53. The other echoes every 'if', to make clear the sections of John's speech and his evasive tone.

c Make it clearer (lines 58–64). One person speaks the lines, the other echoes every mention of Arthur.

d The order (line 66)! In a single line, John makes his intention quite clear. Experiment with different ways of speaking the line (fast, slow with pauses, with John avoiding Hubert's gaze, and so on).

After your explorations, work out how you would stage lines 19–69. Write guidance notes for the actors.

---

keep inhabit, appear in
conceit imagination, thought
troth faith

adjunct consequent, joined
powers reinforcements

Or if that surly spirit, melancholy,
Had baked thy blood and make it heavy-thick,
Which else runs tickling up and down the veins,
Making that idiot, laughter, keep men's eyes   45
And strain their cheeks to idle merriment –
A passion hateful to my purposes –
Or if that thou couldst see me without eyes,
Hear me without thine ears, and make reply
Without a tongue, using conceit alone,   50
Without eyes, ears, and harmful sounds of words;
Then, in despite of broad-eyed watchful day,
I would into thy bosom pour my thoughts.
But, ah, I will not! Yet I love thee well,
And by my troth, I think thou lov'st me well.   55

HUBERT   So well that what you bid me undertake,
Though that my death were adjunct to my act,
By heaven, I would do it.

KING JOHN   Do not I know thou wouldst?
Good Hubert, Hubert, Hubert, throw thine eye
On yon young boy. I'll tell thee what, my friend,   60
He is a very serpent in my way,
And wheresoe'er this foot of mine doth tread,
He lies before me. Dost thou understand me?
Thou art his keeper.

HUBERT   And I'll keep him so
That he shall not offend your majesty.   65

KING JOHN   Death.

HUBERT   My lord.

KING JOHN   A grave.

HUBERT   He shall not live.

KING JOHN   Enough.
I could be merry now. Hubert, I love thee.
Well, I'll not say what I intend for thee.
Remember. – Madam, fare you well;
I'll send those powers o'er to your majesty.   70

ELEANOR   My blessing go with thee.

KING JOHN [To Arthur]   For England, cousin, go.
Hubert shall be your man, attend on you
With all true duty. – On toward Calais, ho!

                                                    Exeunt

King Philip compares his situation to the defeat of an armada. He lists his losses: Angiers, Arthur, many friends, unsuccessful attacks on John. Lewis testifies to John's military skills.

1 John: the military hero (in pairs)

King Philip's lines 1–3 may well have evoked a patriotic cheer from the audience at Shakespeare's Globe Theatre. In 1588, only a few years before *King John* was first staged, the mighty armada of Spain had been destroyed as it sought to invade England (and another armada was wrecked in 1596). Lines 5–16 would also have been well received. They portrayed an English king enjoying huge successes in battle against the French, and moving his armies with unparalleled speed and skill.

Either: Write two short articles: one for an English newspaper and one for a French newspaper, telling the events described in lines 1–14.

Or: Imagine you are putting on the play. A friend advises you to cut lines 1–16 because they are too patriotic and praise King John too highly. What do you reply?

2 '*Enter* CONSTANCE'

King Philip describes Constance as someone who reluctantly clings to life. Her body is 'A grave' and a 'vile prison', holding her soul. Advise Constance about how she should appear and speak her first line (line 21), to express her true feelings.

---

flood ocean
armado armada, fleet
consorted sail ships in convoy
run so ill lost the battle (or fled so cowardly)
Divers many
O'erbearing ... France beating off all our attacks

advice disposed military intelligence
temperate order calm under fire
Doth want example has never been seen before
kindred similar
pattern precedent, similar example

ACT 3   SCENE 4
Near Angiers

Enter KING PHILIP, LEWIS THE DAUPHIN, PANDULPH, *attendants*

KING PHILIP So, by a roaring tempest on the flood,
     A whole armado of consorted sail
     Is scattered and disjoined from fellowship.
PANDULPH Courage and comfort. All shall yet go well.
KING PHILIP What can go well when we have run so ill?   5
     Are we not beaten? Is not Angiers lost?
     Arthur ta'en prisoner? Divers dear friends slain?
     And bloody England into England gone,
     O'erbearing interruption spite of France?
LEWIS What he hath won, that hath he fortified.   10
     So hot a speed with such advice disposed,
     Such temperate order in so fierce a cause,
     Doth want example. Who hath read or heard
     Of any kindred action like to this?
KING PHILIP Well could I bear that England had this praise,   15
     So we could find some pattern of our shame.
          Enter CONSTANCE [*with her hair down*]
     Look who comes here! A grave unto a soul,
     Holding th'eternal spirit against her will,
     In the vile prison of afflicted breath.
     I prithee, lady, go away with me.   20
CONSTANCE Lo, now! now see the issue of your peace!
KING PHILIP Patience, good lady, comfort, gentle Constance.

Constance calls on Death to relieve and comfort her. She wishes she could call up Death from his sleep. She denies that she is mad, but wishes she were, to help her forget her grief.

1 Personifying Death (in pairs)

Constance calls lovingly upon Death to relieve her misery. One person reads aloud lines 25–36. The other listens and closely studies the picture on the cover of this edition (which is Death, the fourth horseman of the Apocalypse, from Albrecht Dürer's 'Apocalypse' woodcuts, 1498). Change over and repeat the activity. Afterwards, talk together about how Dürer's image matches (or does not match) Constance's description of Death as that 'fell anatomy' (cruel or fearful skeleton) in line 40.

2 'A modern invocation'

In line 42, Constance says that Death will not listen to 'a modern invocation' (an ordinary person's appeal for help). But her invocation is a powerful ritualistic plea. To express its incantatory nature, speak lines 25–35 aloud, but stress every 'and'. Explore other ways of making Constance's plea sound like an incantation (a spell).

3 'I am not mad'

Constance denies that she is mad, and appeals to Pandulph to 'Preach some philosophy to make me mad' (line 51). Her brain ('My reasonable part') tells her that, if only she were mad, she could forget her son, or think of him only as a rag doll ('babe of clouts').

a Talk together about whether you agree with Pandulph that Constance is uttering 'madness', and not 'sorrow'.

b Constance repeats 'I am not mad' three times (lines 45, 48 and 59). Decide how you think each repetition should be spoken, giving reasons.

---

redress comfort, relief
odoriferous stench fragrant stink
prosperity prosperous people
vaulty empty
household familiar
fulsome nauseating, foul

carrion corpse-eating
buss kiss
belie tell lies about
canonised made a saint
sensible capable, aware

CONSTANCE No, I defy all counsel, all redress,
　　　　　　But that which ends all counsel, true redress:
　　　　　　Death! Death, O amiable, lovely Death,　　　　　　25
　　　　　　Thou odoriferous stench, sound rottenness,
　　　　　　Arise forth from the couch of lasting night,
　　　　　　Thou hate and terror to prosperity,
　　　　　　And I will kiss thy detestable bones,
　　　　　　And put my eyeballs in thy vaulty brows,　　　　　30
　　　　　　And ring these fingers with thy household worms,
　　　　　　And stop this gap of breath with fulsome dust,
　　　　　　And be a carrion monster like thyself.
　　　　　　Come, grin on me, and I will think thou smil'st,
　　　　　　And buss thee as thy wife. Misery's love,　　　　　35
　　　　　　O come to me!
KING PHILIP　　　　　　　O fair affliction, peace.
CONSTANCE No, no, I will not, having breath to cry.
　　　　　　O that my tongue were in the thunder's mouth;
　　　　　　Then with a passion would I shake the world,
　　　　　　And rouse from sleep that fell anatomy　　　　　40
　　　　　　Which cannot hear a lady's feeble voice,
　　　　　　Which scorns a modern invocation.
PANDULPH Lady, you utter madness, and not sorrow.
CONSTANCE Thou art too holy to belie me so.
　　　　　　I am not mad: this hair I tear is mine,　　　　　45
　　　　　　My name is Constance, I was Geoffrey's wife,
　　　　　　Young Arthur is my son, and he is lost.
　　　　　　I am not mad. I would to God I were,
　　　　　　For then 'tis like I should forget myself.
　　　　　　O, if I could, what grief should I forget!　　　　50
　　　　　　Preach some philosophy to make me mad,
　　　　　　And thou shalt be canonised, cardinal,
　　　　　　For, being not mad, but sensible of grief,
　　　　　　My reasonable part produces reason
　　　　　　How I may be delivered of these woes,　　　　　55
　　　　　　And teaches me to kill or hang myself.
　　　　　　If I were mad, I should forget my son,
　　　　　　Or madly think a babe of clouts were he.
　　　　　　I am not mad; too well, too well I feel
　　　　　　The different plague of each calamity.　　　　　60

King Philip orders Constance to bind up her hair. Constance compares this order with the imprisoning of Arthur. She fears that, when she meets Arthur in heaven, he will be utterly changed by sorrow.

Constance, Stratford Memorial Theatre, 1957.

1 Sincere or heartless poetry? (in pairs)

King Philip offers an elaborate image in lines 61–7. He says that Constance's hairs are glued together by tears and so express their sympathy for her loss ('Sticking together in calamity'). Read the lines several times, and decide whether you find them a true expression of Philip's emotions, or whether they feel artificial to you: poetry without a heart.

tresses locks of hair	**Cain** (first son of Adam and Eve)
silver drop tear	**suspire** breathe (was born)
wiry friends hairs	**my bud** (Arthur)
sociable friendly, supporting	**ague's fit** fever attack
bonds hair bands (chains)	**heinous** wicked, sinful
redeem release from captivity	

KING PHILIP   Bind up those tresses. O what love I note
        In the fair multitude of those her hairs,
        Where but by chance a silver drop hath fall'n.
        Even to that drop ten thousand wiry friends
        Do glue themselves in sociable grief,   65
        Like true, inseparable, faithful loves,
        Sticking together in calamity.
CONSTANCE   To England, if you will.
KING PHILIP   Bind up your hairs.
CONSTANCE   Yes, that I will; and wherefore will I do it?
        I tore them from their bonds and cried aloud,   70
        'O that these hands could so redeem my son,
        As they have given these hairs their liberty!'
        But now I envy at their liberty,
        And will again commit them to their bonds,
        Because my poor child is a prisoner.   75
        And father cardinal, I have heard you say
        That we shall see and know our friends in heaven.
        If that be true, I shall see my boy again;
        For since the birth of Cain, the first male child,
        To him that did but yesterday suspire,   80
        There was not such a gracious creature born,
        But now will canker-sorrow eat my bud
        And chase the native beauty from his cheek,
        And he will look as hollow as a ghost,
        As dim and meagre as an ague's fit,   85
        And so he'll die; and rising so again,
        When I shall meet him in the court of heaven
        I shall not know him. Therefore never, never
        Must I behold my pretty Arthur more.
PANDULPH   You hold too heinous a respect of grief.   90
CONSTANCE   He talks to me that never had a son.
KING PHILIP   You are as fond of grief as of your child.

Constance says grief now totally fills up Arthur's place in her life. She leaves, sorrowing. Lewis is moved. Pandulph implies that the recovery of Lewis's fortunes is near.

---

1 Shakespeare's autobiography? (in small groups)

Some people believe that Constance's grieving for Arthur reflects Shakespeare's experience of his wife's sorrow for the death of their young son Hamnet in 1596. Whether or not this is true, lines 93–105 are a moving and powerful expression of a mother's feelings at the loss of her son.

Prepare a presentation of the lines, in a style you think appropriate. You could share out the lines, learn them and speak them varying the tone, pace and feeling. Line 98 could be spoken as a bitterly ironic rebuke to King Philip's line 92.

2 Lewis shows sympathy – for whom?

In Act 3 Scene 1, Lewis gave no comfort to his wife, Blanche, when she was distressed by the terrible dilemma of choosing between her husband and her family. But he seems (lines 107–11) to be genuinely moved by Constance's plight. Do you share this view, or do you think the lines are about the bitterness and shame he feels at his own defeat in battle?

3 A politician gets to work (in pairs)

Pandulph embarks on a plan to revive Lewis's spirits, and to send him again to battle against England. To gather a first impression of Pandulph's methods, take parts and read from line 107 to the end of the scene. Notice how Pandulph begins by twice assuring Lewis that, when things seem at their worst, it is a sign that they will change for the better (lines 112–15, and lines 119–20). Is that a lie, or is there some truth in it?

Remembers reminds	**repair** cure, recovery
Fare you well goodbye	**fit** disease
some outrage (her suicide)	**take leave** are cured
dull ear sleepiness	

CONSTANCE   Grief fills the room up of my absent child,
        Lies in his bed, walks up and down with me,
        Puts on his pretty looks, repeats his words,   95
        Remembers me of all his gracious parts,
        Stuffs out his vacant garments with his form.
        Then have I reason to be fond of grief?
        Fare you well; had you such a loss as I,
        I could give better comfort than you do.   100
        I will not keep this form upon my head, [*Tears her hair*]
        When there is such disorder in my wit.
        O Lord! my boy, my Arthur, my fair son!
        My life, my joy, my food, my all the world!
        My widow-comfort, and my sorrows' cure!   *Exit* 105
KING PHILIP   I fear some outrage, and I'll follow her.   *Exit*
LEWIS   There's nothing in this world can make me joy,
        Life is as tedious as a twice-told tale,
        Vexing the dull ear of a drowsy man;
        And bitter shame hath spoiled the sweet world's taste, 110
        That it yields nought but shame and bitterness.
PANDULPH   Before the curing of a strong disease,
        Even in the instant of repair and health,
        The fit is strongest. Evils that take leave,
        On their departure most of all show evil.   115
        What have you lost by losing of this day?
LEWIS   All days of glory, joy, and happiness.
PANDULPH   If you had won it, certainly you had.
        No, no; when Fortune means to men most good,
        She looks upon them with a threat'ning eye.   120
        'Tis strange to think how much King John hath lost
        In this which he accounts so clearly won.
        Are not you grieved that Arthur is his prisoner?
LEWIS   As heartily as he is glad he hath him.

Pandulph predicts how Lewis will become England's king: John will kill Arthur; Lewis can claim the throne through Blanche; the English will support him, revolted by Arthur's murder.

1 A political lesson

Pandulph identifies a number of political principles, as he prophesies how Lewis can overthrow King John and succeed to the throne of England:

lines 135–6	Those who become kings by illegal means ('snatched', 'unruly') must use violence to maintain their position ('boist'rously maintained')
lines 137–8	Such a wrongdoer ('he that stands upon a slipp'ry place') will use any means, however evil ('vile hold'), to stay in place
lines 147–8	Anyone who kills a legitimate king ('true blood') will always be insecure, because his subjects will revolt
lines 149–52	The killing of Arthur will so appal the people of England that they will support anyone who has the slightest claim to the throne ('none so small advantage shall step forth')
lines 153–9	Natural events will be seen as symbolic omens ('presages') of Heaven's condemnation of John, calling for vengeance for Arthur's murder.

Consider each of the five principles above in turn, and invent a short title or description for each. For example, the first could be 'Usurpers must rule by force'.

2 Women lose out: husbands inherit

Pandulph urges Lewis to claim the throne of England through Blanche. Page 96 shows how that claim could be made.

---

blood emotions
rub obstacle
misplaced usurping
Makes nice ... up will use any evil method to stay in power
lays you plots plots to your advantage

steeps ... blood murders rightful heirs to be safe
so small advantage however slight his claim to be king
check challenge
exhalation shooting star
Abortives monstrous births

PANDULPH Your mind is all as youthful as your blood.   125
        Now hear me speak with a prophetic spirit,
        For even the breath of what I mean to speak
        Shall blow each dust, each straw, each little rub
        Out of the path which shall directly lead
        Thy foot to England's throne. And therefore mark: 130
        John hath seized Arthur, and it cannot be
        That whiles warm life plays in that infant's veins,
        The misplaced John should entertain an hour,
        One minute, nay, one quiet breath of rest.
        A sceptre snatched with an unruly hand,   135
        Must be as boist'rously maintained as gained,
        And he that stands upon a slipp'ry place,
        Makes nice of no vile hold to stay him up.
        That John may stand, then Arthur needs must fall;
        So be it, for it cannot be but so.   140
LEWIS But what shall I gain by young Arthur's fall?
PANDULPH You, in the right of Lady Blanche your wife,
        May then make all the claim that Arthur did.
LEWIS And lose it, life and all, as Arthur did.
PANDULPH How green you are and fresh in this old world!   145
        John lays you plots; the times conspire with you,
        For he that steeps his safety in true blood,
        Shall find but bloody safety, and untrue.
        This act so evilly borne shall cool the hearts
        Of all his people and freeze up their zeal   150
        That none so small advantage shall step forth
        To check his reign but they will cherish it;
        No natural exhalation in the sky,
        No scope of nature, no distempered day,
        No common wind, no customèd event,   155
        But they will pluck away his natural cause
        And call them meteors, prodigies, and signs,
        Abortives, presages, and tongues of heaven,
        Plainly denouncing vengeance upon John.

Pandulph predicts that, when Lewis invades England, John will kill Arthur. The English, incensed by Arthur's death and the Bastard's ransacking of the Church, will revolt against John and welcome Lewis.

1 Bloodstained hands

Design the image that lines 167–8 suggest to you.

2 Pandulph – true or false? (in pairs)

Read aloud Pandulph's lines 125–81, a sentence at a time. At the end of each statement, say whether or not you think he is speaking the truth.

3 'Better matter breeds': devious language?

The Bastard is obviously carrying out King John's orders (lines 171–3) and giving great offence to the Church ('Offending charity'). That, says Pandulph, together with the death of Arthur, will cause the English to flock to Lewis when he invades.

Some critics have argued that Pandulph uses two words which imply deceit. They say that 'call' (line 174) may not just be a trumpet call, but could also be the decoy call of a bird hunter, to lure ('train') the English support for Lewis. Decide whether you think these interpretations of 'call' and 'train' are unduly sophisticated, intended to cast Pandulph in an unfavourable light.

4 'Strange actions'

In line 182, 'strange' might mean 'strong', 'foolish', 'foreign' (invade England), 'unexpected' or 'unusual'. Give reasons for saying which of these possibilities you prefer.

---

gone dead
unacquainted change unknown
  new man: Lewis (also a
  personification of 'change')
matter of reasons for

hurly tumult
matter breeds things are
  happening
wrought made
whet on spur, sharpen

ACT 4   SCENE 1
The Tower of London

Enter HUBERT *and* EXECUTIONERS *with irons and rope*

HUBERT   Heat me these irons hot, and look thou stand
    Within the arras. When I strike my foot
    Upon the bosom of the ground, rush forth
    And bind the boy which you shall find with me
    Fast to the chair. Be heedful; hence, and watch.   5
EXECUTIONER   I hope your warrant will bear out the deed.
HUBERT   Uncleanly scruples! Fear not you; look to't.
                                 [Executioners withdraw]
    Young lad, come forth; I have to say with you.

Enter ARTHUR

ARTHUR   Good morrow, Hubert.
HUBERT   Good morrow, little prince.
ARTHUR   As little prince, having so great a title   10
    To be more prince, as may be. You are sad.
HUBERT   Indeed I have been merrier.
ARTHUR   Mercy on me!
    Methinks nobody should be sad but I:
    Yet I remember, when I was in France,
    Young gentlemen would be as sad as night,   15
    Only for wantonness. By my christendom,
    So I were out of prison and kept sheep,
    I should be as merry as the day is long,
    And so I would be here but that I doubt
    My uncle practises more harm to me.   20
    He is afraid of me, and I of him.
    Is it my fault that I was Geoffrey's son?
    No, indeed, is't not, and I would to God
    I were your son, so you would love me, Hubert.

Hubert fears that his sympathy will be aroused if he does not act quickly.
He shows Arthur the warrant. Arthur reminds Hubert that he nursed
him in sickness.

---

1 'I warrant' (in pairs)

In line 31, Arthur tells Hubert, 'I warrant (am sure) I love you more
than you do me'. Hubert's 'warrant' to blind Arthur makes Arthur's
word 'warrant' full of irony. Take parts and read lines 9–36,
emphasising Hubert's reactions to Arthur's unawareness of what lies
in store for him. What might happen at line 33?

2 The warrant

Earlier, King John and Hubert agreed that Arthur should be killed.
Write your own version of the warrant.

3 Another anachronism: 'handkercher'

The handkerchief ('handkercher', line 42) is another anachronism.
Handkerchiefs were unknown in King John's day, and were rare in
Shakespeare's. As late as the nineteenth century they were still
uncommon, and therefore valuable. (In Dickens's *Oliver Twist*, Fagin
tells his gang of pickpockets to steal handkerchiefs.) A handkerchief
'wrought' (made) by 'a princess' (line 43) would be a significant gift.
See page 6 for an activity on anachronisms.

4 'Crafty love' (in pairs)

In line 53, Arthur talks of 'crafty love', love which was not genuine but
a pretence, serving Arthur's self-interest. His 'cunning' echoes the idea
of 'Commodity' which runs through the play. To find an appropriate
tone of voice for Arthur, one person reads lines 41–58 as sincerely as
possible, and the other in a 'crafty' way. How do you think Arthur
should speak; is he crafty or sincere?

---

prate talk	**knit** tied
sudden quick, ruthless	**Still and anon** often, continually
sooth faith	**'What lack you?'** what do you
take possession of my bosom	want?
touch my heart	**grief** pain
rheum tears	**love** (line 49) deed
dispiteous cruel	**lien** lain

HUBERT *[Aside]* If I talk to him with his innocent prate   25
       He will awake my mercy, which lies dead;
       Therefore I will be sudden, and dispatch.
ARTHUR Are you sick, Hubert? You look pale today.
       In sooth, I would you were a little sick,
       That I might sit all night and watch with you.   30
       I warrant I love you more than you do me.
HUBERT *[Aside]* His words do take possession of my bosom. –
       Read here, young Arthur. *[Shows the warrant]*
                [Aside]   How now, foolish rheum?
       Turning dispiteous torture out of door?
       I must be brief, lest resolution drop   35
       Out of mine eyes in tender womanish tears. –
       Can you not read it? Is it not fair writ?
ARTHUR Too fairly, Hubert, for so foul effect:
       Must you with hot irons burn out both mine eyes?
HUBERT Young boy, I must.
ARTHUR   And will you?
HUBERT   And I will.   40
ARTHUR Have you the heart? When your head did but ache,
       I knit my handkercher about your brows
       (The best I had, a princess wrought it me)
       And I did never ask it you again;
       And with my hand at midnight held your head;   45
       And like the watchful minutes to the hour,
       Still and anon cheered up the heavy time,
       Saying, 'What lack you?' and 'Where lies your grief?'
       Or 'What good love may I perform for you?'
       Many a poor man's son would have lien still,   50
       And ne'er have spoke a loving word to you;
       But you at your sick-service had a prince.
       Nay, you may think my love was crafty love,
       And call it cunning. Do, and if you will.
       If heaven be pleased that you must use me ill,   55
       Why then you must. Will you put out mine eyes?
       These eyes that never did nor never shall
       So much as frown on you?
HUBERT   I have sworn to do it,
       And with hot irons must I burn them out.

Arthur cannot believe that Hubert will blind him. Hubert summons the executioners, but Arthur begs for them to be sent away. Hubert orders them out and prepares to blind Arthur.

1 Iron

Arthur talks of an 'iron age' (times that are very cruel) and develops an elaborate personification:

lines 61–4 Although 'red-hot', the iron would 'drink' (absorb) Arthur's tears. Its fierce heat would be extinguished, either because of the fact ('matter') that he is innocent, or by the tears themselves.

lines 65–6 The iron would then be eaten away by rust, because it had contained fire to harm Arthur's eyes. The lines are an intricate conceit (image). In the theatre, an audience may gain only a general sense of the personification, but a reader of the play can pause to think about the precise detail.

Using line 67 as an opening, write two more lines in the same style, to extend the personification of iron.

2 Action! (in groups of four)

Lines 67–70 are a personal appeal to Hubert. The stage directions in line 71 show what happens. Take parts as Hubert, Arthur and the executioners. Read lines 67–76 slowly, and work out what actions would accompany the words. Decide which are most effective.

3 Compassionate executioners? (in pairs)

Line 85 and Arthur's talk of the executioner's 'gentle heart' and 'compassion' stand in contrast to the 'iron age' of King John's cruelty.

Explore different ways of speaking line 85. Is the executioner relieved, compassionate, or feeling some other emotion?

---

boist'rous-rough violent
Thrust send
torment torture

chid away driven away with harsh words
Give life to awaken
remedy alternative

ARTHUR Ah, none but in this iron age would do it.   60
        The iron of itself, though heat red-hot,
        Approaching near these eyes, would drink my tears
        And quench his fiery indignation
        Even in the matter of mine innocence;
        Nay, after that, consume away in rust   65
        But for containing fire to harm mine eye.
        Are you more stubborn-hard than hammered iron?
        And if an angel should have come to me
        And told me Hubert should put out mine eyes,
        I would not have believed him – no tongue but Hubert's.   70
HUBERT [*Stamps*] Come forth.
        [*Executioners come forward with rope, irons, etc.*]
                  Do as I bid you do.
ARTHUR O save me, Hubert, save me! My eyes are out
        Even with the fierce looks of these bloody men.
HUBERT Give me the iron, I say, and bind him here.
ARTHUR Alas, what need you be so boist'rous-rough?   75
        I will not struggle, I will stand stone-still.
        For God's sake, Hubert, let me not be bound!
        Nay hear me, Hubert; drive these men away,
        And I will sit as quiet as a lamb.
        I will not stir nor wince nor speak a word   80
        Nor look upon the iron angerly.
        Thrust but these men away, and I'll forgive you,
        Whatever torment you do put me to.
HUBERT Go stand within; let me alone with him.
EXECUTIONER I am best pleased to be from such a deed.   85
                  [*Exeunt Executioners*]

ARTHUR Alas, I then have chid away my friend!
        He hath a stern look but a gentle heart.
        Let him come back, that his compassion may
        Give life to yours.
HUBERT   Come, boy, prepare yourself.
ARTHUR Is there no remedy?
HUBERT   None but to lose your eyes.   90

Arthur pleads not to be blinded. He argues that the irons and fire are cold, because they are unwilling to harm him. Hubert capitulates; not even all of John's wealth would make him blind Arthur.

Hubert threatens to blind Arthur. Arthur pleads that, just as the irons and fire have gone cold, so any object Hubert used would refuse to harm him. Instead, the objects would turn on Hubert, as a badly-abused dog would turn on its cruel master. Throughout this scene, Arthur appeals to Hubert by name, to try to make him merciful. Check how many times Arthur says 'Hubert', and think about the effect created by such repetition of the name. Does Arthur say the name the same way each time?

mote speck of dust	**Snatch** snap
boist'rous painful	**tarre** urge
want pleading lack power to plead	**Deny their office** refuse to act
repentant ashes sorrowing ashes	**Creatures of note** objects known
(like a religious penitent who seeks	**owes** owns
forgiveness)	**purpose** intend
sparkle send sparks	

ARTHUR   O God, that there were but a mote in yours,
         A grain, a dust, a gnat, a wandering hair,
         Any annoyance in that precious sense;
         Then feeling what small things are boist'rous there,
         Your vile intent must needs seem horrible.   95
HUBERT   Is this your promise? Go to, hold your tongue.
ARTHUR   Hubert, the utterance of a brace of tongues
         Must needs want pleading for a pair of eyes.
         Let me not hold my tongue, let me not, Hubert,
         Or Hubert, if you will, cut out my tongue,   100
         So I may keep mine eyes. O spare mine eyes,
         Though to no use but still to look on you.
         Lo, by my troth, the instrument is cold
         And would not harm me.
HUBERT   I can heat it, boy.
ARTHUR   No, in good sooth. The fire is dead with grief,   105
         Being create for comfort, to be used
         In undeserved extremes. See else yourself,
         There is no malice in this burning coal;
         The breath of heaven hath blown his spirit out
         And strewed repentant ashes on his head.   110
HUBERT   But with my breath I can revive it, boy.
ARTHUR   And if you do, you will but make it blush
         And glow with shame of your proceedings, Hubert.
         Nay, it perchance will sparkle in your eyes,
         And like a dog that is compelled to fight,   115
         Snatch at his master that doth tarre him on.
         All things that you should use to do me wrong
         Deny their office. Only you do lack
         That mercy which fierce fire and iron extends,
         Creatures of note for mercy-lacking uses.   120
HUBERT   Well see to live; I will not touch thine eye,
         For all the treasure that thine uncle owes.
         Yet am I sworn, and I did purpose, boy,
         With this same very iron to burn them out.
ARTHUR   O now you look like Hubert. All this while   125
         You were disguisèd.

Hubert will follow the dangerous course of telling John that Arthur is dead. John has been crowned for a second time, which Pembroke and Salisbury say is unnecessary and excessive.

1 'You are dead'

Hubert will pretend that he obeyed King John's order to kill Arthur. He will give 'false reports' (line 128) to John's 'dogged (cruel) spies'. Imagine you are Hubert and write:

- a version of the conversation you will have with the 'spies'.
- an entry for your private diary telling, truthfully, what happened and why.

2 John's second coronation (in small groups)

Show the ceremony. Most stage productions of *King John* open Scene 2 with the ceremony of King John's second crowning. Work out how you would stage your version. Think particularly about how John would behave. Is he confident, nervous, unsure, or has he some other reaction? His behaviour should explain how he speaks his two opening lines. Also consider how the barons react.

3 'Wasteful and ridiculous excess'

Lines 11–16 are some of the most famous and memorable in the play. Salisbury reflects on the futility of attempting to better that which is already perfect.

They are the ideal lines to say when asked to do something which you feel is unnecessary! Devise a method to help someone learn these lines. For some people, simple repetition is effective. Others prefer a visual cue in a series of pictures based on the lines. A sung version sticks in other minds. How would you do it? Can you prove the effectiveness of your method?

---

doubtless without worries
closely secretly
high royalty regal status
plucked off removed

double pomp two ceremonies
with taper-light ... garnish to add to the beauty of the sun with a candle

HUBERT   Peace, no more. Adieu.
          Your uncle must not know but you are dead.
          I'll fill these dogged spies with false reports,
          And, pretty child, sleep doubtless and secure
          That Hubert, for the wealth of all the world,   130
          Will not offend thee.
ARTHUR   O God! I thank you, Hubert.
HUBERT Silence, no more. Go closely in with me.
          Much danger do I undergo for thee.

                                                    Exeunt

ACT 4   SCENE 2
London   King John's palace

Enter KING JOHN in pomp, crowned, PEMBROKE, SALISBURY,
  BIGOT and other barons. KING JOHN sits on the throne

KING JOHN Here once again we sit, once again crowned
          And looked upon, I hope, with cheerful eyes.
PEMBROKE This 'once again', but that your highness pleased,
          Was once superfluous: you were crowned before,
          And that high royalty was ne'er plucked off,   5
          The faiths of men ne'er stainèd with revolt;
          Fresh expectation troubled not the land
          With any longed-for change or better state.
SALISBURY Therefore, to be possessed with double pomp,
          To guard a title that was rich before,   10
          To gild refinèd gold, to paint the lily,
          To throw a perfume on the violet,
          To smooth the ice or add another hue
          Unto the rainbow, or with taper-light
          To seek the beauteous eye of heaven to garnish,   15
          Is wasteful and ridiculous excess.

The barons express concern that the change from tradition will be a source of trouble. John promises that he will explain his reasons. He is willing to listen to requests for reform.

1 You often mar what you strive to mend (in pairs)

The barons object to King John's second coronation. John was, in fact, crowned at least four times during his reign.

Many of the proverbs used by Pembroke and Salisbury tell of people's reluctance to accept change. In lines 23–4, Salisbury uses a metaphor of sailing to explain the dangers of change. If a boat is following one course, a 'shifted' wind (changing direction) will cause a boat 'to fetch about' (change tack), which is a risky manoeuvre.

In lines 28–34, Pembroke points out the dangers of trying too hard to patch up faults and thereby making them worse. His use of the word 'fault' (line 30) could be a reference to John's faulty claim to the throne.

Talk together about why the barons greet change with suspicion, and why change is often greeted with suspicion today.

2 The barons' attitude (in pairs)

'Doth make a stand at what your highness will.' Salisbury's line 39 could have different interpretations (seeming to support or challenge King John). Are the barons in this scene:

- practising Commodity
- asserting themselves over the king
- doing both?

Talk together about which seems most likely.

---

unseasonable inappropriate
this this action (the coronation)
well-noted familiar
old form custom, tradition
frights consideration frightens
  people into asking questions
confound spoil
covetousness greed

excusing hiding
breach tear, rip
breathed our counsel gave advice
  discreetly
overbear over-rule
possessed informed
indue provide

PEMBROKE But that your royal pleasure must be done,
This act is as an ancient tale new told,
And, in the last repeating, troublesome,
Being urgèd at a time unseasonable.   20
SALISBURY In this the antique and well-noted face
Of plain old form is much disfigurèd,
And like a shifted wind unto a sail,
It makes the course of thoughts to fetch about,
Startles and frights consideration,   25
Makes sound opinion sick and truth suspected
For putting on so new a fashioned robe.
PEMBROKE When workmen strive to do better than well,
They do confound their skill in covetousness,
And oftentimes excusing of a fault   30
Doth make the fault the worser by th'excuse.
As patches set upon a little breach
Discredit more in hiding of the fault
Than did the fault before it was so patched.
SALISBURY To this effect, before you were new crowned   35
We breathed our counsel; but it pleased your highness
To overbear it, and we are all well pleased,
Since all and every part of what we would
Doth make a stand at what your highness will.
KING JOHN Some reasons of this double coronation   40
I have possessed you with, and think them strong.
And more, more strong, when lesser is my fear,
I shall indue you with. Meantime, but ask
What you would have reformed that is not well,
And well shall you perceive how willingly   45
I will both hear and grant you your requests.

Pembroke asks for Arthur's release; his imprisonment is causing rumours and opposition. John agrees. Hubert whispers to John. Pembroke suspects that Arthur has been killed by Hubert.

1 'Dangerous argument'

Pembroke, in line 55, again seems to be voicing misgivings as to the validity of King John's claim to the throne. He argues that dissidents ('the time's enemies') are claiming that, if John's claim is valid, there is no need for Arthur to be imprisoned. In lines 61–6, he emphasises that the welfare ('weal') of the king depends on his subjects, just as their well-being relies on him.

Read lines 47–66. Firstly, as a responsible, reasonable man doing his duty for his country. Secondly, read them in a very threatening manner. Does one way sound more convincing than the other?

2 Simile and metaphor

The effect of Hubert's message on King John is reflected in Salisbury's lines 76–9. He first uses a simile comparing the changes of colour in John's face. Pleasure and guilt follow each other, like heralds going between two rival armies ('battles'). He then uses a metaphor of sickness. John's crime is being revealed, like a ripe boil bursting and releasing 'corruption' (pus). Notice how Pembroke extends the metaphor in lines 80–1.

---

tongue spokesperson	**good exercise** education
Bend their best studies direct their strongest efforts	**To grace occasions** give backing to attacks
enfranchisement setting free	**suit** plea
rest peace	**goods** advantages
attend/The steps follow the path	**direction** safe-keeping
mew up imprison	**close aspect** guilty look

PEMBROKE   Then I – as one that am the tongue of these
            To sound the purposes of all their hearts,
            Both for myself and them, but chief of all,
            Your safety, for the which myself and them   50
            Bend their best studies – heartily request
            Th'enfranchisement of Arthur, whose restraint
            Doth move the murmuring lips of discontent
            To break into this dangerous argument:
            If what in rest you have in right you hold,   55
            Why then your fears – which, as they say, attend
            The steps of wrong – should move you to mew up
            Your tender kinsman and to choke his days
            With barbarous ignorance and deny his youth
            The rich advantage of good exercise?   60
            That the time's enemies may not have this
            To grace occasions, let it be our suit
            That you have bid us ask, his liberty,
            Which for our goods we do no further ask
            Than whereupon our weal, on you depending,   65
            Counts it your weal he have his liberty.

                  Enter HUBERT

KING JOHN   Let it be so. I do commit his youth
            To your direction. – Hubert, what news with you?
              [Hubert whispers to the King]
PEMBROKE   This is the man should do the bloody deed.
            He showed his warrant to a friend of mine.   70
            The image of a wicked heinous fault
            Lives in his eye; that close aspect of his
            Doth show the mood of a much troubled breast,
            And I do fearfully believe 'tis done
            What we so feared he had a charge to do.   75
SALISBURY   The colour of the king doth come and go
            Between his purpose and his conscience,
            Like heralds 'twixt two dreadful battles set.
            His passion is so ripe it needs must break.
PEMBROKE   And when it breaks, I fear will issue thence   80
            The foul corruption of a sweet child's death.

John announces Arthur's death. The barons hold him responsible, and leave threatening trouble. John realises that murder brings insecurity. A Messenger brings news: the French have invaded.

1 'Arthur is deceased' (in groups of three)

The news that Arthur died the night before evokes a strong reaction from Salisbury and Pembroke. Take parts and read lines 82–105. Will the barons be ironic, sarcastic, directly accusing, or speak in some other way?

2 'The shears of destiny'

King John denies he has the power to control death. In classical mythology, 'the shears of destiny' (line 91) were used by Atropos, one of the three Fates (controllers of human lives), to cut the thread of life spun and woven by the other two Fates. Draw the image that John's words suggest to you.

3 Stage the barons' departure

Pembroke, Salisbury and the other barons leave with accusing and threatening words. Work out how they would exit, showing their reaction to what has happened.

4 Levels of irony (in groups of five)

Irony is present throughout this scene because of the different perceptions involved about Arthur's 'death'. Take parts as Salisbury, Pembroke, King John and two members of the audience. Each character states clearly what he knows or believes to be the truth about Arthur's death, and his reaction to this 'fact'. The two audience members tell each character the true story, and talk about their response to what the character has said.

---

hold stop
commandment control
greatness one in authority
grossly obviously
owed owned
breadth whole
ere before

set built
certain sure
foreign preparation invasion force
levied raised
in the body of throughout
copy model

KING JOHN [*Coming forward*] We cannot hold mortality's strong hand.
      Good lords, although my will to give is living,
      The suit which you demand is gone and dead.
      He tells us Arthur is deceased tonight.   85
SALISBURY Indeed we feared his sickness was past cure.
PEMBROKE Indeed we heard how near his death he was,
      Before the child himself felt he was sick.
      This must be answered either here or hence.
KING JOHN Why do you bend such solemn brows on me?   90
      Think you I bear the shears of destiny?
      Have I commandment on the pulse of life?
SALISBURY It is apparent foul-play, and 'tis shame
      That greatness should so grossly offer it.
      So thrive it in your game! and so farewell.   95
PEMBROKE Stay yet, Lord Salisbury. I'll go with thee
      And find th'inheritance of this poor child,
      His little kingdom of a forcèd grave.
      That blood which owed the breadth of all this isle,
      Three foot of it doth hold; bad world the while!   100
      This must not be thus borne, this will break out
      To all our sorrows, and ere long, I doubt.
                            Exeunt [*lords*]
KING JOHN They burn in indignation. I repent.
      There is no sure foundation set on blood,
      No certain life achieved by others' death.   105

Enter MESSENGER

      A fearful eye thou hast. Where is that blood
      That I have seen inhabit in those cheeks?
      So foul a sky clears not without a storm,
      Pour down thy weather: how goes all in France?
MESSENGER From France to England. Never such a power   110
      For any foreign preparation
      Was levied in the body of a land.
      The copy of your speed is learned by them,
      For when you should be told they do prepare,
      The tidings comes that they are all arrived.   115

The Messenger announces the deaths of Eleanor and Constance, and reports that Lewis commands the French army. The Bastard reports he has extorted money from the Church and that the people are fearful.

1 Questions, questions (in pairs)

Take parts as King John and the Messenger and read lines 116–31. Try different tones and styles for the two characters (the punctuation marks provide helpful clues).

2 The Bastard's entrance (in pairs)

King John is reeling from the Messenger's news as the Bastard enters. The Bastard rebukes John (lines 135–6), saying that, if he is frightened of bad news, then he deserves the consequences of living in ignorance. Work out ways to play lines 131–46. Make as clear as possible the effect that the Bastard's intervention has on John.

3 Personification

The opposite page contains a number of personifications:

line 116 'intelligence': military intelligence is pictured as being asleep or drunk

line 123 'rumour': the death of Constance and Eleanor is reported by 'rumour's tongue'

line 125 'Occasion': John begs Fate to stay on his side until he and the barons are reconciled

line 128 'estate': John's lands in France are pictured as walking wildly

line 132 'world': the people, reacting to the Bastard's mission, are seen as the world talking.

You will find more information on personification on page 182.

---

intelligence military information, spies
frenzy fit
Withhold cease
Occasion Fate, Fortune
peers barons

conduct command
proceedings mission
amazed totally overwhelmed
Aloft above
strangely fantasied full of strange ideas

KING JOHN   O, where hath our intelligence been drunk?
        Where hath it slept? Where is my mother's care?
        That such an army could be drawn in France,
        And she not hear of it?
MESSENGER   My liege, her ear
        Is stopped with dust: the first of April died   120
        Your noble mother; and as I hear, my lord,
        The Lady Constance in a frenzy died
        Three days before; but this from rumour's tongue
        I idly heard – if true or false I know not.
KING JOHN   Withhold thy speed, dreadful Occasion!   125
        O, make a league with me till I have pleased
        My discontented peers. What? Mother dead?
        How wildly then walks my estate in France!
        Under whose conduct came those powers of France
        That thou for truth giv'st out are landed here?   130
MESSENGER   Under the Dauphin.

Enter BASTARD *and* PETER OF POMFRET

KING JOHN   Thou hast made me giddy
        With these ill tidings. – Now, what says the world
        To your proceedings? Do not seek to stuff
        My head with more ill news, for it is full.
BASTARD   But if you be afeared to hear the worst,   135
        Then let the worst, unheard, fall on your head.
KING JOHN   Bear with me, cousin, for I was amazed
        Under the tide, but now I breathe again
        Aloft the flood and can give audience
        To any tongue, speak it of what it will.   140
BASTARD   How I have sped among the clergymen
        The sums I have collected shall express,
        But as I travelled hither through the land,
        I find the people strangely fantasied,
        Possessed with rumours, full of idle dreams,   145
        Not knowing what they fear, but full of fear.

*Peter of Pomfret has prophesied that John will cease to be king on
Ascension Day. John orders Peter to be hanged on that day.
The Bastard is sent to bring the barons quickly to John.*

'Foreknowing that the truth will fall out so.' Peter of Pomfret prophesies
that King John will give up his crown on Ascension Day. John orders Peter
to be imprisoned and hanged at noon on that day.

Pomfret Pontefract (in Yorkshire)
treading on his heels following
 closely
Foreknowing because I knew before
tonight last night
the better foot before as fast as
 possible

subject enemies enemies who are
 my subjects
adverse hostile
Mercury messenger of the gods
sprightful brave

And here's a prophet that I brought with me
From forth the streets of Pomfret, whom I found
With many hundreds treading on his heels,
To whom he sung in rude harsh-sounding rhymes,   150
That ere the next Ascension Day at noon,
Your highness should deliver up your crown.
KING JOHN Thou idle dreamer, wherefore didst thou so?
PETER Foreknowing that the truth will fall out so.
KING JOHN Hubert, away with him; imprison him,   155
And on that day at noon, whereon he says
I shall yield up my crown, let him be hanged.
Deliver him to safety and return,
For I must use thee.
                                    [*Exit Hubert with Peter*]
                         O my gentle cousin,
Hear'st thou the news abroad, who are arrived?   160
BASTARD The French, my lord; men's mouths are full of it.
Besides, I met Lord Bigot and Lord Salisbury
With eyes as red as new-enkindled fire,
And others more, going to seek the grave
Of Arthur, whom they say is killed tonight   165
On your suggestion.
KING JOHN   Gentle kinsman, go
And thrust thyself into their companies;
I have a way to win their loves again.
Bring them before me.
BASTARD   I will seek them out.
KING JOHN Nay, but make haste; the better foot before.   170
O, let me have no subject enemies
When adverse foreigners affright my towns
With dreadful pomp of stout invasion.
Be Mercury, set feathers to thy heels,
And fly like thought from them to me again.   175
BASTARD The spirit of the time shall teach me speed.   *Exit*
KING JOHN Spoke like a sprightful noble gentleman.
Go after him, for he perhaps shall need
Some messenger betwixt me and the peers,
And be thou he.
MESSENGER   With all my heart, my liege.   [*Exit*] 180

John recalls his mother's death. Hubert tells of the English people's fears at the five moons, Arthur's death and the French invasion. John tries to blame Hubert for the death of Arthur.

1 A soliloquy for John

Line 181 is a soliloquy (see page 16). Using this line as a beginning, write a soliloquy of twelve lines for King John to speak at this point.

2 In the streets (in groups of four to eight)

Hubert tells that the 'five moons' are seen as omens of trouble to come. In lines 185–202, he paints a vivid picture of the ordinary people's reactions to the disturbing events that are taking place. Re-create the scene with words and actions. First, talk about the lines to share your ideas. Then one person slowly reads the lines, while the others act out each element of Hubert's description. (To help you: 'beldams' = old women; 'measure' = tailor's ruler; 'artificer' = workman.)

3 Like father, like son?

It was allegedly the words, 'Who will rid me of this turbulent priest?', spoken by King Henry II, King John's father, that led three of Henry's knights to kill Thomas à Becket in Canterbury Cathedral. Henry later argued that it was a simple cry of frustration from a king, not an order. Nevertheless, Henry did penance for the murder. John is trying to use the same technique, saying that Hubert must have misinterpreted 'the winking of authority' (taken a hint that wasn't intended). He blames servants for mistaking a king's 'humour' (whim) for a command with the strength of a 'warrant' (the legal authority to act).

---

wondrous strange
dangerously as being dangerous, in a way that is dangerous
fearful action gestures of fear
contrary wrong
embattailèd in position for battle

humours moods, whims
warrant authority to act
bloody house of life the human body
advised respect deliberate thought

KING JOHN My mother dead!

Enter HUBERT

HUBERT My lord, they say five moons were seen tonight:
   Four fixèd, and the fift did whirl about
   The other four in wondrous motion.
KING JOHN Five moons?
HUBERT   Old men and beldams in the streets 185
   Do prophesy upon it dangerously.
   Young Arthur's death is common in their mouths,
   And when they talk of him, they shake their heads,
   And whisper one another in the ear.
   And he that speaks doth gripe the hearer's wrist, 190
   Whilst he that hears makes fearful action
   With wrinkled brows, with nods, with rolling eyes.
   I saw a smith stand with his hammer, thus,
   The whilst his iron did on the anvil cool,
   With open mouth swallowing a tailor's news, 195
   Who, with his shears and measure in his hand,
   Standing on slippers, which his nimble haste
   Had falsely thrust upon contrary feet,
   Told of a many thousand warlike French
   That were embattailèd and ranked in Kent. 200
   Another lean, unwashed artificer
   Cuts off his tale and talks of Arthur's death.
KING JOHN Why seek'st thou to possess me with these fears?
   Why urgest thou so oft young Arthur's death?
   Thy hand hath murdered him. I had a mighty cause 205
   To wish him dead, but thou hadst none to kill him.
HUBERT No had, my lord? Why, did you not provoke me?
KING JOHN It is the curse of kings to be attended
   By slaves that take their humours for a warrant
   To break within the bloody house of life, 210
   And on the winking of authority
   To understand a law, to know the meaning
   Of dangerous majesty, when perchance it frowns
   More upon humour than advised respect.

Hubert shows the death warrant with John's signature. John accepts that he will be judged in Heaven, but blames Hubert for looking like a murderer and not showing dissent. John bemoans his fate.

1 The last account

When he sees his signature and seal on the death warrant, King John at first admits that it is evidence that would damn him on Judgement Day ('the last account 'twixt heaven and earth'), but he tries to absolve himself by implicating Hubert more and more. Lines 219–41 could be read as John's defence on the Day of Judgement. He makes the following statements (but not in this order):

a But you took my hints literally and responded too quickly

b I barely hinted of Arthur's death to you

c If only you had spoken against the murder. If only you had asked me to be explicit, I'd have been shamed to silence

d So you did it, though neither of us spoke directly

e Seeing evil things prompts people to do evil

f You did it to gain favour with a king

g You had the look of someone who would willingly do evil

h Your fears would have stopped me.

Re-arrange the statements into the order in which John uses them.

2 Unfair temptation? (in small groups)

'How oft the sight of means to do ill deeds/Make deeds ill done!' In lines 219–20, King John says that if opportunities to do wrong exist, people will do wrong. Do you agree with his judgement?

---

means a way
marked,/Quoted, and
 signed picked out
abhorred aspect ugly face
faintly broke lightly hinted
darkly indirectly

express explicit
stop pause
held thought
braved challenged
in the body of this fleshly land
 in my own body

HUBERT Here is your hand and seal for what I did.   215
               [*Shows the warrant*]
KING JOHN O, when the last account 'twixt heaven and earth
        Is to be made, then shall this hand and seal
        Witness against us to damnation!
        How oft the sight of means to do ill deeds
        Make deeds ill done! Hadst not thou been by,   220
        A fellow by the hand of nature marked,
        Quoted, and signed to do a deed of shame,
        This murder had not come into my mind.
        But taking note of thy abhorred aspect,
        Finding thee fit for bloody villainy,   225
        Apt, liable to be employed in danger,
        I faintly broke with thee of Arthur's death,
        And thou, to be endearèd to a king,
        Made it no conscience to destroy a prince.
HUBERT My lord –   230
KING JOHN Hadst thou but shook thy head or made a pause
        When I spake darkly what I purposèd,
        Or turned an eye of doubt upon my face,
        As bid me tell my tale in express words,
        Deep shame had struck me dumb, made me break off,   235
        And those thy fears might have wrought fears in me.
        But thou didst understand me by my signs
        And didst in signs again parley with sin,
        Yea, without stop, didst let thy heart consent,
        And consequently thy rude hand to act   240
        The deed which both our tongues held vile to name.
        Out of my sight, and never see me more!
        My nobles leave me, and my state is braved,
        Even at my gates, with ranks of foreign powers.
        Nay, in the body of this fleshly land,   245
        This kingdom, this confine of blood and breath,
        Hostility and civil tumult reigns
        Between my conscience and my cousin's death.

Hubert advises John to fight. Because Arthur lives, John's conscience can be cleared. John orders him to tell the barons, so that they will return to loyalty. He apologises to Hubert.

1 'More hideous than thou art' (in pairs)

References to Hubert's ugliness are made throughout the play. King John is particularly insulting in this scene. In line 224, he talks of Hubert's 'abhorred aspect' (hateful appearance). Even when apologising for remarks about Hubert's looks, he still manages to be rude. He says that it was rage ('eyes of blood') that made him see Hubert as even 'more hideous than thou art'. Line 266 often makes the audience laugh.

a How would you answer an actor who objected to being made up to look very unattractive to play the part?

   Turn to pages 97, 104, 135 and 152 to see how Hubert has been presented in stage productions.

b In *Macbeth*, Shakespeare expresses a different view of the relationship between appearance and reality, when Duncan states, 'There's no art / To find the mind's construction in the face' (Act 1 Scene 4, lines 11–12). Do you think a person's looks can reveal their character?

2 'Doth Arthur live?'

Compare King John's reaction to the news that Arthur lives (lines 260–2) with what he said in lines 103–5. Are there any similarities in the responses? Do they give an indication of John's real feelings?

3 Production notes

Imagine you are directing the play. In your production, what would prompt King John to say, 'O, answer not!' (line 267)?

---

a maiden unstained
bosom mind
motion idea
rude exteriorly ugly outside
tame calm, acquiescent

feature appearance, face
imaginary imagining
closet private room
conjure urge

HUBERT   Arm you against your other enemies;
        I'll make a peace between your soul and you.   250
        Young Arthur is alive. This hand of mine
        Is yet a maiden and an innocent hand,
        Not painted with the crimson spots of blood.
        Within this bosom never entered yet
        The dreadful motion of a murderous thought   255
        And you have slandered nature in my form,
        Which howsoever rude exteriorly,
        Is yet the cover of a fairer mind
        Than to be butcher of an innocent child.
KING JOHN   Doth Arthur live? O, haste thee to the peers,   260
        Throw this report on their incensèd rage,
        And make them tame to their obedience!
        Forgive the comment that my passion made
        Upon thy feature, for my rage was blind,
        And foul imaginary eyes of blood   265
        Presented thee more hideous than thou art.
        O, answer not! but to my closet bring
        The angry lords with all expedient haste.
        I conjure thee but slowly; run more fast.

                                        Exeunt [*severally*]

Arthur, disguised, tries to escape, but dies in the attempt. Salisbury,
Pembroke and Bigot plan to meet Lewis, who has promised friendship.
The Bastard asks them to meet John.

---

1 The death of Arthur (in pairs)

Arthur knows he faces certain death if he stays, so is willing to take the
risk of death in an escape (line 8). His escape bid fails.

a Work out how you would stage Arthur's leap. In the theatre, it
sometimes causes the audience to laugh. How would you avoid
this happening?

b Talk together about why Arthur might have chosen to disguise
himself as a ship-boy. Then design Arthur's costume.

c Line 10 is similar to the opening sentence of wills made at the
time of Elizabeth I. How do you think Arthur should speak it?

2 History into drama (in small groups)

Shakespeare was a playwright, not an historian. He was concerned
with dramatic effect, rather than strict historical fact (see page 177).
In Scene 3, he takes liberties with time and place: Arthur died in
1203, but the barons did not meet at Bury St Edmunds ('Saint
Edmundsbury') until 1214, and Lewis was not there. Shakespeare
also makes Arthur's death an accident. No one knows for sure how
Arthur died, but many believe that King John had him murdered.

Write a dialogue between an historian and Shakespeare, in which
they argue over whether or not a playwright should accurately portray
historical events. Base it on Scene 3.

Alternatively, you could work in groups, divided into 'historians'
and 'playwrights' and have a debate on the subject.

---

semblance appearance, clothing
shifts tricks (or other disguises)
privity private communication
general wide-ranging in friendship
import tell

set forward let's leave now
or ere before
distempered ill-tempered
straight immediately

ACT 4 SCENE 3
The Tower of London

Enter ARTHUR *on the walls (disguised as a ship-boy)*

ARTHUR   The wall is high, and yet will I leap down.
    Good ground, be pitiful and hurt me not.
    There's few or none do know me; if they did,
    This ship-boy's semblance hath disguised me quite.
    I am afraid, and yet I'll venture it.   5
    If I get down and do not break my limbs,
    I'll find a thousand shifts to get away.
    As good to die and go, as die and stay.
            [Leaps down]
    O me, my uncle's spirit is in these stones.
    Heaven take my soul, and England keep my bones.   *Dies*   10

Enter PEMBROKE, SALISBURY, *and* BIGOT

SALISBURY   Lords, I will meet him at Saint Edmundsbury;
    It is our safety, and we must embrace
    This gentle offer of the perilous time.
PEMBROKE   Who brought that letter from the cardinal?
SALISBURY   The Count Melun, a noble lord of France,   15
    Whose privity with me o'th'Dauphin's love
    Is much more general than these lines import.
BIGOT   Tomorrow morning let us meet him then.
SALISBURY   Or rather then set forward, for 'twill be
    Two long days' journey, lords, or ere we meet.   20

Enter BASTARD

BASTARD   Once more today well met, distempered lords!
    The king by me requests your presence straight.

The barons refuse to support John. Seeing Arthur's body, they condemn his death as the wickedest of all murders. The Bastard questions whether Arthur has been murdered.

1 Bloodstained John

Salisbury's lines 24–6 conjure up an image of King John in a bloodstained cloak and leaving bloody footprints. Sketch your design ideas for a theatre programme cover, based on these lines.

2 Personifying murder and ...

a Lines 37–8 personify murder as hating what it does, and so urging revenge for its own bloody act. There are several other personifications opposite. Identify the human characteristics associated with death, wrath, rage and remorse.

b Decide whether you think the Bastard also personifies impatience in line 33.

3 Sincerity? (in groups of three)

Take parts as Salisbury, Pembroke and Bigot and read lines 34–56 several times. Afterwards, talk together about whether you think that the barons are grieving sincerely for Arthur, or whether they have other motives for speaking as they do.

4 'If ...'

Advise the Bastard about how to deliver line 59, in which he questions whether Arthur has in fact been murdered. For example, the Bastard might inspect the body, or heavily stress 'If', or have a long pause before he speaks. What does this line suggest about his character?

---

dispossessed deprived
line reinforce
good words courtesy
reason (line 29) speak, are in
  control
beheld seen
vildest vilest

wall-eyed glaring
remorse pity
sole unique
yet-unbegotten yet to be conceived
heinous wicked
graceless godless

SALISBURY The king hath dispossessed himself of us,
We will not line his thin bestainèd cloak
With our pure honours, nor attend the foot   25
That leaves the print of blood where'er it walks.
Return, and tell him so. We know the worst.
BASTARD Whate'er you think, good words I think were best.
SALISBURY Our griefs and not our manners reason now.
BASTARD But there is little reason in your grief.   30
Therefore 'twere reason you had manners now.
PEMBROKE Sir, sir, impatience hath his privilege.
BASTARD 'Tis true – to hurt his master, no man else.
SALISBURY This is the prison. [Sees Arthur] What is he lies here?
PEMBROKE O death made proud with pure and princely beauty!   35
The earth had not a hole to hide this deed.
SALISBURY Murder, as hating what himself hath done,
Doth lay it open to urge on revenge.
BIGOT Or when he doomed this beauty to a grave,
Found it too precious-princely for a grave.   40
SALISBURY Sir Richard, what think you? Have you beheld,
Or have you read or heard? or could you think,
Or do you almost think, although you see,
That you do see? Could thought, without this object,
Form such another? This is the very top,   45
The height, the crest, or crest unto the crest
Of murder's arms. This is the bloodiest shame,
The wildest savagery, the vildest stroke
That ever wall-eyed wrath or staring rage
Presented to the tears of soft remorse.   50
PEMBROKE All murders past do stand excused in this,
And this, so sole and so unmatchable,
Shall give a holiness, a purity,
To the yet-unbegotten sin of times,
And prove a deadly bloodshed but a jest,   55
Exampled by this heinous spectacle.
BASTARD It is a damnèd and a bloody work,
The graceless action of a heavy hand –
If that it be the work of any hand.

King John

Salisbury and the barons swear an oath of revenge for Arthur's death.
Hubert arrives to say that Arthur lives, but is threatened by Salisbury.
Hubert defends his innocence.

1 Swearing the oath (in small groups)

Work out how to stage the swearing of the oath in lines 62–73.
Experiment with ways of making the words and actions very like those
of a religious ritual. Decide whether, in line 71, Salisbury indicates his
own or Arthur's hand.

Royal Shakespeare Company, 1974. Hubert is kneeling over Arthur's body.
The Bastard (centre) will challenge Salisbury (second left, with drawn
sword). *King John* was written long before *Othello*, but line 79 seems to
forecast Othello's words, 'Put up your bright swords or the dew will rust
them', when he faces a group of men with drawn swords.
Decide at which point in the script opposite you think Hubert first
sees Arthur's dead body.

We had … ensue we guessed what
would happen
practice evil scheming, plot
breathless dead
incense homage (like incense
offered in a religious ceremony)

conversant in contact
set a glory to glorified
Avaunt clear off!
marking of seeing only

SALISBURY If that it be the work of any hand?   60
          We had a kind of light what would ensue.
          It is the shameful work of Hubert's hand,
          The practice and the purpose of the king,
          From whose obedience I forbid my soul,
          Kneeling before this ruin of sweet life,   65
          And breathing to his breathless excellence
          The incense of a vow, a holy vow,
          Never to taste the pleasures of the world,
          Never to be infected with delight
          Nor conversant with ease and idleness,   70
          Till I have set a glory to this hand,
          By giving it the worship of revenge.
PEMBROKE⎫
           ⎬ Our souls religiously confirm thy words.
BIGOT   ⎭

              Enter HUBERT

HUBERT Lords, I am hot with haste in seeking you.
          Arthur doth live, the king hath sent for you.   75
SALISBURY O, he is bold, and blushes not at death! –
          Avaunt, thou hateful villain, get thee gone!
HUBERT I am no villain.
SALISBURY   Must I rob the law? [*Draws*]
BASTARD Your sword is bright, sir; put it up again.
SALISBURY Not till I sheathe it in a murderer's skin.   80
HUBERT Stand back, Lord Salisbury, stand back I say!
          By heaven, I think my sword's as sharp as yours.
          I would not have you, lord, forget yourself,
          Nor tempt the danger of my true defence,
          Lest I, by marking of your rage, forget   85
          Your worth, your greatness, and nobility.
BIGOT Out, dunghill! Dar'st thou brave a nobleman?
HUBERT Not for my life, but yet I dare defend
          My innocent life against an emperor.
SALISBURY Thou art a murderer.
HUBERT   Do not prove me so;   90
          Yet I am none. Whose tongue soe'er speaks false,
          Not truly speaks; who speaks not truly, lies.

The Bastard defends Hubert. The barons disbelieve Hubert's claim of innocence, and leave to join Lewis at Bury St Edmunds. The Bastard says that Hubert will be eternally damned if he killed Arthur.

1 True colours

Why does the Bastard defend Hubert so strongly? He takes Hubert's side against the barons, and defies Salisbury's threats and insults (Salisbury calls him 'Falconbridge' rather than 'Sir Richard').

At the end of Act 2, the Bastard swore to follow self-interest ('Commodity'), but now he stands up for fairness. He will not condemn a man without evidence, even though very powerful forces are against him. See page 181 for more on the Bastard's character.

2 'Nothing is so black' – politically incorrect?

Imagine you are directing the play. The actor playing the Bastard says to you: 'I feel very uncomfortable about saying line 121. It may have been OK in Shakespeare's time to equate blackness with evil, but you just can't do that today. It's offensive. Can't we cut the line?' What do you reply?

3 Social class

Shakespeare makes Hubert of lower social class than the barons. By the 'code of honour' of the times, a nobleman would not duel with a person of lower social rank, but would simply kill him. The tradition was also that persons of lower social class would not dream of fighting with a nobleman.

Identify all the words in lines 74–110 which suggest Hubert's lower social status. Advise the actors about how to deliver them with appropriate contempt or defiance.

---

gall hurt, wound
hasty spleen quick anger
do me shame insult me
betime instantly
toasting-iron sword
Second support

date of life out until I die
rheum tears
abhor hate
Lucifer Satan (angel who fell from Heaven to Hell)

PEMBROKE Cut him to pieces.

BASTARD [*Drawing*]   Keep the peace, I say.

SALISBURY Stand by, or I shall gall you, Falconbridge.

BASTARD Thou wert better gall the devil, Salisbury.   95
    If thou but frown on me, or stir thy foot,
    Or teach thy hasty spleen to do me shame,
    I'll strike thee dead. Put up thy sword betime,
    Or I'll so maul you and your toasting-iron,
    That you shall think the devil is come from hell.   100

BIGOT What wilt thou do, renownèd Falconbridge,
    Second a villain and a murderer?

HUBERT Lord Bigot, I am none.

BIGOT   Who killed this prince?

HUBERT 'Tis not an hour since I left him well.
    I honoured him, I loved him and will weep   105
    My date of life out for his sweet life's loss.

SALISBURY Trust not those cunning waters of his eyes,
    For villainy is not without such rheum;
    And he, long traded in it, makes it seem
    Like rivers of remorse and innocency.   110
    Away with me, all you whose souls abhor
    Th'uncleanly savours of a slaughter-house,
    For I am stifled with this smell of sin.

BIGOT Away toward Bury, to the Dauphin there!

PEMBROKE There, tell the king, he may enquire us out.   115

Exeunt lords

BASTARD Here's a good world. Knew you of this fair work?
    Beyond the infinite and boundless reach
    Of mercy, if thou didst this deed of death,
    Art thou damned, Hubert.

HUBERT Do but hear me, sir –

BASTARD   Ha! I'll tell thee what.   120
    Thou'rt damned as black – nay nothing is so black –
    Thou art more deep damned than Prince Lucifer.
    There is not yet so ugly a fiend of hell
    As thou shalt be, if thou didst kill this child.

Faced with the Bastard's suspicions, Hubert swears that he is innocent of Arthur's death in thought, word and deed. The Bastard decides to support John in the troubled and uncertain days ahead.

1 'Vast confusion waits'

The Bastard, watching Hubert lift up Arthur ('How easy dost thou take all England up!'), expresses and echoes the uncertainties and confusion ('thorns and dangers') of the times. Decide which of the following interpretations you prefer. You might decide that more than one interpretation is valid in each case.

lines 144–5 'The life, the right, and truth of all this realm/Is fled to heaven.' Does the Bastard say this about Arthur, or the state of England – or both?

line 147 'The unowed interest of proud-swelling state.' Does the Bastard mean 'the loyalty owed to kings', or 'the illegally owned ('unowed') possessions of John'?

lines 151–2 'Powers from home and discontents at home/Meet in one line.' This might mean 'civil war threatens as rival groups meet head on', or 'Lewis's army ('powers from home') and the barons ('discontents') join together to fight us'. Which would you choose?

line 154 'The imminent decay of wrested pomp.' This could mean 'The coming overthrow of John's usurped ('wrested') authority', or 'The approaching struggle over whether John or Lewis should be king'. Which do you prefer?

Some people still argue fiercely over the interpretation of the Bastard's words. But all agree that they embody the uncertainties and difficulties of the time. So don't think you have to come to a final, unambiguous conclusion about their meaning. But every production does have to decide how the actor will deliver them!

---

cord hangman's rope
rush thin reed
embounded enclosed
this beauteous clay Arthur's body
want lack

scamble fight over
dogged war (a personification, with at least three images!)
centure belt

HUBERT Upon my soul —
BASTARD   If thou didst but consent   125
　　　To this most cruel act, do but despair,
　　　And if thou want'st a cord, the smallest thread
　　　That ever spider twisted from her womb
　　　Will serve to strangle thee; a rush will be a beam
　　　To hang thee on. Or wouldst thou drown thyself,   130
　　　Put but a little water in a spoon,
　　　And it shall be as all the ocean,
　　　Enough to stifle such a villain up.
　　　I do suspect thee very grievously.
HUBERT If I in act, consent, or sin of thought,   135
　　　Be guilty of the stealing that sweet breath
　　　Which was embounded in this beauteous clay,
　　　Let hell want pains enough to torture me!
　　　I left him well.
BASTARD   Go, bear him in thine arms.
　　　I am amazed, methinks, and lose my way   140
　　　Among the thorns and dangers of this world.
　　　How easy dost thou take all England up!
　　　From forth this morsel of dead royalty,
　　　The life, the right, and truth of all this realm
　　　Is fled to heaven; and England now is left   145
　　　To tug and scamble and to part by th'teeth
　　　The unowed interest of proud-swelling state.
　　　Now for the bare-picked bone of majesty,
　　　Doth dogged war bristle his angry crest
　　　And snarleth in the gentle eyes of peace.   150
　　　Now powers from home and discontents at home
　　　Meet in one line, and vast confusion waits
　　　As doth a raven on a sick-fall'n beast,
　　　The imminent decay of wrested pomp.
　　　Now happy he, whose cloak and centure can   155
　　　Hold out this tempest. Bear away that child,
　　　And follow me with speed. I'll to the king.
　　　A thousand businesses are brief in hand,
　　　And heaven itself doth frown upon the land.

　　　　　　　　　　　　　　　　　　　　　Exeunt

Looking back at Act 4

Activities for groups or individuals

1 The barons

Salisbury, Pembroke and Bigot are called 'barons' throughout this edition, even though Shakespeare refers to them as 'lords'. The historical events in which they were involved in King John's reign are now known as the 'Barons' Revolt'. The most famous moment was when the barons forced John to sign Magna Carta at Runnymede in 1215. In Scene 2, line 168, John claims that, although the barons are angry, 'I have a way to win their loves again'. Is Shakespeare hinting at Magna Carta? Imagine that John continues with four lines, saying what he has in mind to conciliate the barons. Write the four lines.

2 John, son of Eleanor

King John first hears the news of his mother's death in Scene 2, line 120. Later, when he is alone on stage, he recalls his loss: 'My mother dead!' (line 181). Nicholas Woodeson, the actor who played John in the Royal Shakespeare Company's 1988 production, took these words as a clue to discover John's character. Talk together about how you think Queen Eleanor's life and death influences John.

3 Plot the events

In *King John*, Shakespeare was not concerned to present an accurate historical account (see page 177). He compresses time and events. To help gain a sense of time in Act 4, identify the main events and draw a time scale to plot when each one happens.

4 Rhyme

Each scene in Act 4 ends with a rhyming couplet (two lines which rhyme). Turn to the end of each scene, to remind yourself of the lines. Suggest reasons why you think Shakespeare chose to close the scenes in this way, and advise the actors how you think the lines should be spoken. For example, should the rhymes be emphasised?

Arthur's story. These four pictures show Arthur's progress through the play. Fiercely protected by his mother, Constance, he is then captured and threatened with blinding by Hubert. He tries to escape, but his leap to freedom ends in his death, and his body is lifted up by Hubert. Find suitable captions from the script for each picture.

If you go to Stratford-upon-Avon, look at the mural high up on the wall of the Swan Theatre in Waterside. It shows Arthur pleading not to be blinded.

John yields the crown to Pandulph, who returns it as a symbol of the Pope's authority. Pandulph says that he will fulfil his promise to stop the French, because John is now the Pope's subject.

Pandulph crowns King John. Here are two versions of the stage direction at line 3. John has been forced to eat his words of defiance. He now submits to the Pope's authority. Talk together about what you think lies behind each director's presentation of this moment in the play.

holding leasehold
holy word solemn vow
his holiness the Pope (contrast John's words at 3.1.149–71)
inflamed engulfed
counties barons or shires

obedience authority
stranger foreign
mistempered humour illness
Rests remains
overthrow incurable death
convertite new convert

ACT 5   SCENE 1
London   King John's palace

Enter KING JOHN and PANDULPH, attendants

KING JOHN [*Giving the crown*] Thus have I yielded up into your hand
    The circle of my glory. [*Kneels*]
PANDULPH [*Places crown upon John's head*] Take again
    From this my hand, as holding of the Pope,
    Your sovereign greatness and authority.
KING JOHN Now keep your holy word: go meet the French,   5
    And from his holiness use all your power
    To stop their marches 'fore we are inflamed.
    Our discontented counties do revolt;
    Our people quarrel with obedience,
    Swearing allegiance and the love of soul   10
    To stranger blood, to foreign royalty.
    This inundation of mistempered humour
    Rests by you only to be qualified.
    Then pause not, for the present time's so sick
    That present med'cine must be ministered,   15
    Or overthrow incurable ensues.
PANDULPH It was my breath that blew this tempest up,
    Upon your stubborn usage of the Pope,
    But since you are a gentle convertite,
    My tongue shall hush again this storm of war   20
    And make fair weather in your blust'ring land.
    On this Ascension Day, remember well,
    Upon your oath of service to the Pope,
    Go I to make the French lay down their arms.   *Exit*

John recalls the prophecy. The Bastard reports that Kent and London have yielded. Only Dover Castle resists. The barons have joined the French. Arthur is dead. The Bastard urges strong action.

1 John's reactions (in pairs)

a Remind yourself of Peter of Pomfret's prophecy and King John's reaction to it (Act 4 Scene 2, lines 151–7). Work out how you would advise John to speak lines 25–9. For example, is he cowardly, despairing, relieved, or expressing some other emotion? Does he speak to the audience, the attendants or to himself?

b 'But wherefore do you droop?' The news of Arthur's death seems to have a profound effect on John. Follow the clues in the script, and work out what physical reaction the actor playing John might make to the Bastard's news.

2 Stirring into action (in pairs)

The Bastard makes a stirring speech on how a king should act in war (lines 45–61). He attempts to lift King John's spirits and turn him into a mighty military leader. The king should 'Be stirring' (active) and 'outface' (challenge) those who threaten 'horror'. His example should inspire 'inferior eyes' (the sight of his subjects), and he should 'become' (honour) the battlefield with his presence. The Bastard refers to 'the lion in his den', to remind John both of the symbol of England and Richard Cœur-de-lion. Notice that the Bastard issues at least a dozen instructions on how John should behave (for example, 'Be great', 'Let not').

Is the Bastard really talking to John, or is he making an appeal to an audience or mentally preparing himself to do great deeds?

Try whispering the lines in your partner's ear. Then stand far apart and shout them. Try them as a radio broadcast to the nation. Which presentation do you think is the most effective?

---

on constraint by force
powers troops
aught all
Govern rule
aspiring hopeful

Forage ravage (hunt for prey)
displeasure hostility
ere he come so nigh before he
  comes near

KING JOHN Is this Ascension Day? Did not the prophet   25
    Say that before Ascension Day at noon
    My crown I should give off? Even so I have.
    I did suppose it should be on constraint.
    But, heav'n be thanked, it is but voluntary.

Enter BASTARD

BASTARD All Kent hath yielded; nothing there holds out   30
    But Dover Castle. London hath received,
    Like a kind host, the Dauphin and his powers.
    Your nobles will not hear you, but are gone
    To offer service to your enemy,
    And wild amazement hurries up and down   35
    The little number of your doubtful friends.
KING JOHN Would not my lords return to me again
    After they heard young Arthur was alive?
BASTARD They found him dead and cast into the streets,
    An empty casket, where the jewel of life   40
    By some damned hand was robbed and ta'en away.
KING JOHN That villain Hubert told me he did live.
BASTARD So, on my soul, he did, for aught he knew.
    But wherefore do you droop? Why look you sad?
    Be great in act, as you have been in thought.   45
    Let not the world see fear and sad distrust
    Govern the motion of a kingly eye.
    Be stirring as the time, be fire with fire,
    Threaten the threat'ner, and outface the brow
    Of bragging horror. So shall inferior eyes,   50
    That borrow their behaviours from the great,
    Grow great by your example and put on
    The dauntless spirit of resolution.
    Away, and glister like the god of war
    When he intendeth to become the field.   55
    Show boldness and aspiring confidence.
    What, shall they seek the lion in his den,
    And fright him there? and make him tremble there?
    O, let it not be said! Forage, and run
    To meet displeasure farther from the doors,   60
    And grapple with him ere he come so nigh.

John admits to his deal with Pandulph. The Bastard condemns any treaty with Lewis. John gives the Bastard command of the army. Lewis orders a copy to be made of the barons' oath of allegiance.

1 'Your peace'

The Bastard pours scorn on King John's appeasement (lines 65–76). His first dislike is for the tactic. It is an 'inglorious league' (a shameful treaty), based on 'fair-play orders' (chivalry) to 'arms invasive' (an army of occupation). His second attack is a personal one against Lewis. The enemy are led by a 'beardless boy' who is to be allowed to 'flesh his spirit' (experience his first military action), without 'check' (opposition). Speak lines 65–76, putting as much contempt as possible into your voice. Pick out all the words that you can 'load' with ridicule.

2 The Bastard takes control

In line 77, King John gives the Bastard control of the English resistance: 'Have thou the ordering of this present time'. Invent moves and gestures for the actors at line 77, to make this transfer of power very obvious.

3 The oath of allegiance

Scene 2 is an unhistorical meeting, invented by Shakespeare. In the theatre, the scene usually opens with the barons swearing the oath and signing the treaty. In line 1, 'this' is the oath under which the English barons have sworn to support Lewis. The signatories have celebrated communion ('took the sacrament') together, to seal the vow. Lewis orders copies to be made of the agreement they have signed. In order to help an audience understand the significance of Lewis's lines, suggest how you would stage the opening of Scene 2.

---

footing soil (or invasion)
Insinuation ingratiating proposals
parley discussion
cockered silken wanton spoilt
  over-dressed playboy
brave insult
idly carelessly, uselessly

purpose of defence a will to
  defend
prouder fiercer
precedent draft
fair order reasonable terms
inviolable unbreakable

KING JOHN The legate of the Pope hath been with me,
        And I have made a happy peace with him,
        And he hath promised to dismiss the powers
        Led by the Dauphin.
BASTARD   O inglorious league!   65
        Shall we, upon the footing of our land,
        Send fair-play orders and make compromise,
        Insinuation, parley, and base truce
        To arms invasive? Shall a beardless boy,
        A cockered silken wanton brave our fields,   70
        And flesh his spirit in a warlike soil
        Mocking the air with colours idly spread,
        And find no check? Let us, my liege, to arms.
        Perchance the cardinal cannot make your peace,
        Or if he do, let it at least be said   75
        They saw we had a purpose of defence.
KING JOHN Have thou the ordering of this present time.
BASTARD Away then with good courage! – [*Aside*] Yet I know
        Our party may well meet a prouder foe.

                                                  Exeunt

ACT 5   SCENE 2
Near Bury St Edmunds

Enter, in arms, LEWIS the DAUPHIN, SALISBURY, MELUN,
PEMBROKE, BIGOT, soldiers

LEWIS My Lord Melun, let this be copied out
        And keep it safe for our remembrance;
        Return the precedent to these lords again,
        That having our fair order written down,
        Both they and we, perusing o'er these notes,   5
        May know wherefore we took the sacrament,
        And keep our faiths firm and inviolable.

Salisbury reaffirms the barons' allegiance, but grieves that they must support Lewis against their own people. Salisbury weeps, and wishes that England could join with France to fight common enemies.

1 Salisbury's grief – sincere or false? (in pairs)

Salisbury stresses that the barons' allegiance is their own choice ('A voluntary zeal and an unurgèd faith'). He grieves that they are forced to honour ('grace') the lords of France and follow 'unacquainted colours' (unfamiliar flags). He wishes that the two Christian countries could combine together, not in 'malice' (enmity), but in a 'league' (truce). United, they could fight a crusade on a 'pagan shore' (a non-Christian land).

How genuine are Salisbury's public tears? Take sides, with one person giving as many reasons as possible to support the view that his grief is sincere, and the other arguing that Salisbury is hypocritical and false. It will help if you read lines 8–39 aloud and talk together about:

- vocabulary (pick out words that seem pretentious)
- metaphorical language (consider the images of England as a diseased body, and moving England like a ship)
- rhythm (flowing or broken? suggesting sincerity or falseness?).

2 My country, right or wrong

To fight for another country against your own people is usually seen as treacherous and unpatriotic. But there are circumstances when such an action is justifiable. Is Salisbury a traitor? What do you think?

---

albeit although
contemned condemned
inveterate canker deep-rooted disease
metal sword
Where honourable rescue ... Salisbury! many look to me for help

physic cure
Was were
spot place, stain (disgrace)
Neptune's arms the sea
clippeth embraces
grapple join

SALISBURY Upon our sides it never shall be broken.
　　　　And, noble Dauphin, albeit we swear
　　　　A voluntary zeal and an unurgèd faith   10
　　　　To your proceedings, yet believe me, prince,
　　　　I am not glad that such a sore of time
　　　　Should seek a plaster by contemned revolt
　　　　And heal the inveterate canker of one wound
　　　　By making many. O, it grieves my soul   15
　　　　That I must draw this metal from my side
　　　　To be a widow-maker! O, and there
　　　　Where honourable rescue and defence
　　　　Cries out upon the name of Salisbury!
　　　　But such is the infection of the time   20
　　　　That for the health and physic of our right,
　　　　We cannot deal but with the very hand
　　　　Of stern injustice and confusèd wrong,
　　　　And is't not pity, O my grievèd friends,
　　　　That we, the sons and children of this isle,   25
　　　　Was born to see so sad an hour as this,
　　　　Wherein we step after a stranger, march
　　　　Upon her gentle bosom, and fill up
　　　　Her enemies' ranks – I must withdraw and weep
　　　　Upon the spot of this enforcèd cause –   30
　　　　To grace the gentry of a land remote
　　　　And follow unacquainted colours here?
　　　　What, here? O nation, that thou couldst remove,
　　　　That Neptune's arms, who clippeth thee about,
　　　　Would bear thee from the knowledge of thyself,   35
　　　　And grapple thee unto a pagan shore,
　　　　Where these two Christian armies might combine
　　　　The blood of malice in a vein of league
　　　　And not to spend it so unneighbourly.

Lewis praises Salisbury's nobility, but expresses amazement at his tears.
He comforts Salisbury with the promise of wealth. Pandulph brings news
of John's submission to Rome.

---

1 Lewis flatters and persuades (in pairs)

Lewis uses rhetoric (see page 186) to persuade Salisbury of his
sincerity. He praises Salisbury, then urges him to be a man and
promises a substantial reward for his support:

lines 40–4 praise Salisbury's 'temper' (nature), for dealing with
the conflict between 'compulsion' (what one is forced
to do) and 'respect' (love for England)

lines 45–59 elaborately describe Salisbury's tears

lines 60–4 promise wealth to all the barons who support the
French ('nobles' and 'angels' are echoes of money,
see page 80).

Speak Lewis's lines to your partner in several ways: sincerely, cunningly,
sarcastically, and so on. Then talk together about what impression of
Lewis you gain from his words. How has he changed from his earlier
appearances in the play?

2 Big boys don't cry (in pairs)

Salisbury weeps. Earlier (Act 4 Scene 3, lines 107–10), he scorned
Hubert's tears. Now Lewis uses hyperbole (exaggerated language) to
describe how 'amazed' he was at Salisbury's tears. Lewis claims to be
even more astonished than if he'd seen the sky full of supernatural
signs ('the vaulty top of heaven/Figured quite o'er with burning
meteors').

a Pick out the five words or phrases that Lewis uses instead of
'tears', in lines 45–59.

b Talk together about your opinion of men crying in public.

---

ordinary inundation rain shower	**set** seal
heave throw	**come in** submitted
Commend leave	**stood out** rebelled
giant adult	**metropolis and see** city and
Fortune good luck	diocese
knit unite	

LEWIS A noble temper dost thou show in this,   40
   And great affections wrestling in thy bosom
   Doth make an earthquake of nobility.
   O, what a noble combat hast thou fought
   Between compulsion and a brave respect!
   Let me wipe off this honourable dew,   45
   That silverly doth progress on thy cheeks.
   My heart hath melted at a lady's tears,
   Being an ordinary inundation,
   But this effusion of such manly drops,
   This shower, blown up by tempest of the soul,   50
   Startles mine eyes and makes me more amazed
   Than had I seen the vaulty top of heaven
   Figured quite o'er with burning meteors.
   Lift up thy brow, renownèd Salisbury,
   And with a great heart heave away this storm.   55
   Commend these waters to those baby eyes
   That never saw the giant world enraged,
   Nor met with Fortune other than at feasts,
   Full warm of blood, of mirth, of gossiping.
   Come, come; for thou shalt thrust thy hand as deep   60
   Into the purse of rich prosperity
   As Lewis himself. So, nobles, shall you all,
   That knit your sinews to the strength of mine.
       [Trumpet sounds]
   And even there, methinks an angel spake!

     Enter PANDULPH *[attended]*

   Look where the holy legate comes apace,   65
   To give us warrant from the hand of heaven,
   And on our actions set the name of right
   With holy breath.
PANDULPH   Hail, noble Prince of France.
   The next is this: King John hath reconciled
   Himself to Rome; his spirit is come in,   70
   That so stood out against the holy church,
   The great metropolis and see of Rome.

Pandulph tells Lewis to stop the war. Lewis refuses, saying it was Pandulph who pointed out to him the strength of his claim. Lewis stresses that Rome is not involved, and that he has English support.

1 The lion and the fire (in pairs)

In line 75, Pandulph uses the image of a lion 'fostered up at hand' (hand-reared), and therefore harmless. In lines 83–7, the Dauphin uses the image of a re-kindled fire.

Talk together about which other characters or incidents in the play these images bring to mind.

2 Rhetorical questions (in groups of three)

In lines 91–107, Lewis asks a series of rhetorical questions (not requiring answers; said for effect). One person reads the questions, pausing after each. The others answer as Pandulph might have done, had he been given the opportunity.

3 'Vive le roi!'

'*Vive le roi*' ('Long live the king') is also a card-playing term. Lines 103–7 are an extended metaphor on card playing:

'crown' = a sum of money or stake

'yielded set' = to win the first hand of cards

'banked' = to win, to add to the bank.

Lewis's use of the word 'banked' could mean that the citizens cheered Lewis, as he won their support and took their towns. It could also mean that they shouted their support, as he sailed past the river banks of the towns. Which interpretation do you prefer?

---

threat'ning colours battle banners
propertied treated as an inferior
instrument agent
breath words
matter fuel
face of right recognise my rights

interest claim
munition arms
underprop support
liable subject
outside surface
work problem

Therefore thy threat'ning colours now wind up
And tame the savage spirit of wild war,
That like a lion fostered up at hand,   75
It may lie gently at the foot of peace
And be no further harmful than in show.
LEWIS Your grace shall pardon me, I will not back.
I am too high-born to be propertied,
To be a secondary at control,   80
Or useful servingman and instrument
To any sovereign state throughout the world.
Your breath first kindled the dead coal of wars
Between this chastised kingdom and myself
And brought in matter that should feed this fire,   85
And now 'tis far too huge to be blown out
With that same weak wind which enkindled it.
You taught me how to know the face of right,
Acquainted me with interest to this land,
Yea, thrust this enterprise into my heart;   90
And come ye now to tell me John hath made
His peace with Rome? What is that peace to me?
I, by the honour of my marriage-bed,
After young Arthur, claim this land for mine;
And now it is half-conquered, must I back   95
Because that John hath made his peace with Rome?
Am I Rome's slave? What penny hath Rome borne?
What men provided? What munition sent
To underprop this action? Is't not I
That undergo this charge? Who else but I,   100
And such as to my claim are liable,
Sweat in this business and maintain this war?
Have I not heard these islanders shout out
Vive le roi! as I have banked their towns?
Have I not here the best cards for the game   105
To win this easy match played for a crown?
And shall I now give o'er the yielded set?
No, no, on my soul, it never shall be said.
PANDULPH You look but on the outside of this work.

Lewis determines to continue the war. The Bastard, as John's ambassador, asks for news. He greets Lewis's defiance with pleasure, and paints a glowing picture of John's military skill.

1 From diplomacy to war (in pairs)

The Bastard's tone changes. In lines 118–23, he is formal and polite. When he learns of the forthcoming war, he becomes defiant and challenging (lines 127–58). Talk together about how an actor might deliver the lines. For example, think about the violent verbs and strong visual images the Bastard uses to describe King John's treatment of the French (lines 131–53).

The rhetoric of war. The language used by the Bastard as he describes the military power of King John, finds an echo in every age. This 1917 German poster is typical of the images and language used to inspire soldiers and citizens alike. (Translation: This is the way to peace – the enemy wills it so! Therefore subscribe to the War Loan!)

ample hope high ambition	**unadvisèd revel** unwise game
head of war army	**unhaired** youthful
culled collected	**at your door** in France
outlook search for (or defy)	**hatch** exit doors
warrant authority	**litter** straw for animals
temporise come to terms with	**nation's crow** cockerel (emblem of
harnessed armoured	France)

LEWIS Outside or inside, I will not return   110
          Till my attempt so much be glorified
          As to my ample hope was promisèd
          Before I drew this gallant head of war
          And culled these fiery spirits from the world
          To outlook conquest and to win renown   115
          Even in the jaws of danger and of death.
                        [*Trumpet sounds*]
          What lusty trumpet thus doth summon us?

                        Enter BASTARD

BASTARD According to the fair play of the world,
          Let me have audience; I am sent to speak,
          My holy lord of Milan, from the king: 120
          I come to learn how you have dealt for him,
          And, as you answer, I do know the scope
          And warrant limited unto my tongue.
PANDULPH The Dauphin is too wilful-opposite
          And will not temporise with my entreaties.   125
          He flatly says, he'll not lay down his arms.
BASTARD By all the blood that ever fury breathed,
          The youth says well! Now hear our English king,
          For thus his royalty doth speak in me:
          He is prepared, and reason too he should.   130
          This apish and unmannerly approach,
          This harnessed masque and unadvisèd revel,
          This unhaired sauciness and boyish troops,
          The king doth smile at, and is well prepared
          To whip this dwarfish war, this pygmy arms   135
          From out the circle of his territories.
          That hand which had the strength, even at your door,
          To cudgel you and make you take the hatch,
          To dive like buckets in concealèd wells,
          To crouch in litter of your stable planks,   140
          To lie like pawns locked up in chests and trunks,
          To hug with swine, to seek sweet safety out
          In vaults and prisons, and to thrill and shake
          Even at the crying of your nation's crow,
          Thinking this voice an armèd Englishman –   145

The Bastard praises John and rebukes the rebel barons. Lewis dismisses the Bastard's boasting and declares war. The Bastard defiantly accepts the challenge and again praises John's military prowess.

1 'Ingrate revolts' (in groups of six)

Some of the Bastard's worst abuse is reserved for the disloyal barons, 'you degenerate, you ingrate revolts' (unnatural, ungrateful rebels). Talk together about how the barons might react to this tirade. Are they defiant, ashamed or unmoved? They may feel many different emotions.

a One person reads aloud the Bastard's lines 148–58. The others react as the barons. Decide how to show your feelings, as the Bastard speaks.

b Decide how allegiance to either King John or Lewis could be expressed by the barons, as they leave the stage.

2 Drums and trumpets

Trumpets are used in the scene to announce the arrival of ambassadors. Drums are a symbol of war. The Bastard (lines 166–78) uses the loudness of a drum as an image of defiance. In stage performances, drums and trumpets may be the only music used. A film or television version could well have a musical score which reflects the varying moods of the scene.

Work through Scene 2, suggesting where music might be effective, and the type of music to be played.

3 A public relations exercise

Everything the Bastard says from line 128 to the end of the scene is intended to create a warlike image of King John. Speak the lines as a radio broadcast designed to raise the morale of the English.

---

chambers cities	**end thy brave** stop boasting
eyrie nest, or brood (eaglets)	**turn thy face** go back to where
tow'rs soars	you came from
souse annoyance attack intruders	**braced** tightened
Neroes refers to the Roman	**welkin's** sky's
emperor who killed his mother	**halting** limping
Amazons female warriors	**office** duty

Shall that victorious hand be feebled here,
That in your chambers gave you chastisement?
No! Know the gallant monarch is in arms
And like an eagle o'er his eyrie tow'rs
To souse annoyance that comes near his nest.   150
And you degenerate, you ingrate revolts,
You bloody Neroes, ripping up the womb
Of your dear mother England, blush for shame!
For your own ladies and pale-visaged maids,
Like Amazons, come tripping after drums,   155
Their thimbles into armèd gauntlets change,
Their needles to lances and their gentle hearts
To fierce and bloody inclination.
LEWIS There end thy brave, and turn thy face in peace;
We grant thou canst outscold us. Fare thee well;   160
We hold our time too precious to be spent
With such a brabbler.
PANDULPH   Give me leave to speak.
BASTARD No, I will speak.
LEWIS   We will attend to neither.
Strike up the drums, and let the tongue of war
Plead for our interest and our being here.   165
BASTARD Indeed, your drums being beaten, will cry out;
And so shall you, being beaten. Do but start
An echo with the clamour of thy drum,
And even at hand a drum is ready braced,
That shall reverberate all as loud as thine.   170
Sound but another, and another shall,
As loud as thine, rattle the welkin's ear
And mock the deep-mouthed thunder; for at hand
(Not trusting to this halting legate here,
Whom he hath used rather for sport than need)   175
Is warlike John; and in his forehead sits
A bare-ribbed Death, whose office is this day
To feast upon whole thousands of the French.
LEWIS Strike up our drums to find this danger out.
BASTARD And thou shalt find it, Dauphin, do not doubt.   180

                                        Exeunt

151

A battle is fought. Hubert tells John his forces are losing. A Messenger reports that the French reinforcements have been wrecked and their army retreats. John has a fever and asks to be taken to Swinstead Abbey.

'O, my heart is sick.' Hubert and King John, Royal Shakespeare Company, 1988. The production used a mixture of modern dress and 'period' costume. Throughout his battle campaigns at Angiers and in England, John carried his crown on a cord attached to his belt (see picture).

fares goes
great supply large reinforcements
but even now very recently

coldly dispiritedly
retire retreat
litter stretcher

ACT 5 SCENE 3
A battlefield near Bury St Edmunds

Alarums. Enter KING JOHN *and* HUBERT

KING JOHN How goes the day with us? O, tell me, Hubert.
HUBERT Badly, I fear. How fares your majesty?
KING JOHN This fever that hath troubled me so long
Lies heavy on me. O, my heart is sick.

Enter a MESSENGER

MESSENGER My lord, your valiant kinsman, Falconbridge, 5
Desires your majesty to leave the field,
And send him word by me which way you go.
KING JOHN Tell him toward Swinstead, to the abbey there.
MESSENGER Be of good comfort, for the great supply
That was expected by the Dauphin here 10
Are wrecked three nights ago on Goodwin Sands.
This news was brought to Richard but even now.
The French fight coldly and retire themselves.
KING JOHN Ay me, this tyrant fever burns me up,
And will not let me welcome this good news. 15
Set on toward Swinstead. To my litter straight,
Weakness possesseth me, and I am faint.

Exeunt

The barons fear the battle may go against them. Melun, wounded, urges them to return to John, because Lewis has sworn to execute them if he is victorious.

1 The Bastard in battle (in large groups)

Salisbury tells of the Bastard's military prowess. In spite of all their attacks, the Bastard 'alone' (line 5) is winning victory. Many productions attempt to show just how the Bastard behaves in combat, by inserting a battle scene between Scenes 3 and 4. This gives extra meaning to lines 1–5, because the audience see the English forces, under the Bastard, overcoming the French and the English rebels.

Work out how to stage a battle that can lead to lines 1–5. You could, for example, stage it in several sections: a sequence that leads up to line 1; then a sequence leading to lines 2–3; then a sequence which shows the Bastard's individual exploits, which leads to lines 4–5.

Remember, the golden rule of all stage battles is safety first. The action should look thrillingly dramatic, but should be perfectly safe.

2 'Unthread the rude eye of rebellion'

Melun's line 11 uses the image of unthreading a needle. Decide whether Melun is suggesting that it will be an easy or difficult action for the barons to return to King John (think about whether it is easier to thread or unthread a needle).

Imagine that one of Shakespeare's actors said to him, 'Wouldn't it be better in several ways to say: Unthread the eye of rude rebellion?' What might Shakespeare have replied?

3 Treacherous Lewis

Lewis (the 'He' of line 15) means to execute the English barons after the battle. Why? Suggest three or four likely reasons.

---

stored richly supplied
miscarry fail
In spite of spite defying all our attacks

revolts rebels
bought and sold deceived and betrayed
amity friendship

ACT 5 SCENE 4
The battlefield near Bury St Edmunds

Enter SALISBURY, PEMBROKE and BIGOT

SALISBURY I did not think the king so stored with friends.
PEMBROKE Up once again! Put spirit in the French;
    If they miscarry, we miscarry too.
SALISBURY That misbegotten devil Falconbridge,
    In spite of spite, alone upholds the day.   5
PEMBROKE They say King John, sore sick, hath left the field.

Enter MELUN *wounded [and led by soldiers]*

MELUN Lead me to the revolts of England here.
SALISBURY When we were happy, we had other names.
PEMBROKE It is the Count Melun.
SALISBURY   Wounded to death.
MELUN Fly, noble English, you are bought and sold;   10
    Unthread the rude eye of rebellion,
    And welcome home again discarded faith.
    Seek out King John and fall before his feet,
    For if the French be lords of this loud day,
    He means to recompense the pains you take   15
    By cutting off your heads. Thus hath he sworn,
    And I with him, and many more with me,
    Upon the altar at Saint Edmundsbury,
    Even on that altar, where we swore to you
    Dear amity and everlasting love.   20
SALISBURY May this be possible? May this be true?

Melun says that, being so near to death, he can speak only the truth.
He confirms that Lewis intends to execute the barons.
They resolve to return to John.

'Have I not hideous death within my view.' Melun, close to death, reveals
Lewis's treachery. Melun gives several reasons for warning the English
barons of Lewis's treacherous intentions: being near death he must speak
the truth (so that he can enter Heaven); his friendship with Hubert; his
English ancestry. The English barons, impressed by the sight of a man
clearing his conscience and acknowledging his English ancestry, decide to
resume their former loyalty to King John.

quantity small amount
Resolveth melts (like a wax doll)
hence in the after-life
rated calculated, wicked
grandsire grandfather
In lieu whereof in payment for

beshrew curse
bated subsided
rankness swollen growth (excessive
  ambition)
bounds limits
old right upholding John as king

MELUN Have I not hideous death within my view,
   Retaining but a quantity of life,
   Which bleeds away even as a form of wax
   Resolveth from his figure 'gainst the fire?   25
   What in the world should make me now deceive,
   Since I must lose the use of all deceit?
   Why should I then be false, since it is true
   That I must die here and live hence by truth?
   I say again, if Lewis do win the day,   30
   He is forsworn if e'er those eyes of yours
   Behold another day break in the east.
   But even this night, whose black contagious breath
   Already smokes about the burning crest
   Of the old, feeble, and day-wearied sun –   35
   Even this ill night your breathing shall expire,
   Paying the fine of rated treachery,
   Even with a treacherous fine of all your lives,
   If Lewis by your assistance win the day.
   Commend me to one Hubert with your king;   40
   The love of him, and this respect besides,
   For that my grandsire was an Englishman,
   Awakes my conscience to confess all this.
   In lieu whereof, I pray you bear me hence
   From forth the noise and rumour of the field,   45
   Where I may think the remnant of my thoughts
   In peace, and part this body and my soul
   With contemplation and devout desires.
SALISBURY We do believe thee, and beshrew my soul,
   But I do love the favour and the form   50
   Of this most fair occasion, by the which
   We will untread the steps of damnèd flight,
   And like a bated and retirèd flood,
   Leaving our rankness and irregular course,
   Stoop low within those bounds we have o'erlooked,   55
   And calmly run on in obedience
   Even to our ocean, to our great King John.
   My arm shall give thee help to bear thee hence,
   For I do see the cruel pangs of death
   Right in thine eye. Away, my friends! New flight   60
   And happy newness that intends old right.
          Exeunt [leading off Melun]

Lewis believes that he has won this day's battle against the English.
A Messenger brings news of the shipwreck of Lewis's reinforcements.
He resolves to fight again early tomorrow.

1 French victory? (in small groups)

Consider three different ways for Lewis to speak lines 1–8:

a to the audience in the theatre

b to his army

c to himself.

Identify what differences each would involve, giving specific examples from the lines.

2 Bad news

Another Messenger brings bad news and is cursed for it. Advise the Messenger about how to speak each of his six lines, in the knowledge that such messengers in Shakespeare's plays usually get a rough reception (see page 58).

3 Lewis: a different perspective

If this were the only sight you had of Lewis in the play, how would you assess his character? Find six words to sum up how he appears to you in this scene.

loath reluctant
welkin sky
measure crossed
faint retire cowardly retreat
needless shot unnecessary cannon
 fire
wound ... colours clearly up
 furled our tattered flags

fall'n off deserted
supply reinforcements and
 equipment
shrewd bitter
Beshrew curse
quarter guard

ACT 5   SCENE 5
The battlefield near Bury St Edmunds

LEWIS the DAUPHIN and his army

LEWIS The sun of heaven, methought, was loath to set,
But stayed and made the western welkin blush,
When English measure backward their own ground
In faint retire. O, bravely came we off,
When with a volley of our needless shot,   5
After such bloody toil, we bid good night,
And wound our tott'ring colours clearly up,
Last in the field and almost lords of it!

Enter a MESSENGER

MESSENGER Where is my prince, the Dauphin?
LEWIS   Here: what news?
MESSENGER The Count Melun is slain, the English lords   10
By his persuasion are again fall'n off,
And your supply, which you have wished so long,
Are cast away and sunk on Goodwin Sands.
LEWIS Ah, foul shrewd news! Beshrew thy very heart!
I did not think to be so sad tonight   15
As this hath made me. Who was he that said
King John did fly an hour or two before
The stumbling night did part our weary pow'rs?
MESSENGER Whoever spoke it, it is true, my lord.
LEWIS Well, keep good quarter and good care tonight;   20
The day shall not be up so soon as I
To try the fair adventure of tomorrow.
                                        Exeunt

Hubert and the Bastard meet in the dark night. They do not recognise each other at first. Hubert asks pardon of the Bastard for not recognising him. The Bastard asks for news.

1 Meeting in the dark (in pairs)

Lines 1–9 recall the opening of *Hamlet*. Both scenes depict a similar situation. Two men, meeting in the dark at a time of intense military peril, challenge uneasily, to discover each other's identity. To gain a sense of the wariness of the meeting (and of what happens in the scene), take parts and read lines 1–44.

Afterwards, talk together about how you would play the opening lines on stage, to create the impression of total darkness and the uncertainties of the time. Write detailed notes for the actors.

2 'One way of the Plantagenets'

The Bastard speaks about his royal ancestry in line 11. Some critics believe Shakespeare inserted lines 11 and 38 to show that the Bastard (now the most powerful man on the English side) could be a contender for the throne of England. Do you think that the Bastard will make a bid to become king before the play ends? Make a guess, with reasons, and check if you are right as you read on.

---

part side
perfect correct
upon all hazards at any risk
Unkind remembrance bad memory

eyeless moonless
any accent ... thy tongue your voice
sans compliment without flattery or courtesies

ACT 5   SCENE 6
Night   Near Swinstead Abbey

Enter BASTARD and HUBERT from different directions

HUBERT Who's there? Speak ho! Speak quickly or I shoot.

BASTARD A friend. What art thou?

HUBERT   Of the part of England.

BASTARD Whither dost thou go?

HUBERT   What's that to thee?

BASTARD Why may not I demand of thine affairs,
      As well as thou of mine? –   5
      Hubert, I think.

HUBERT   Thou hast a perfect thought.
      I will upon all hazards well believe
      Thou art my friend that know'st my tongue so well.
      Who art thou?

BASTARD   Who thou wilt; and if thou please
      Thou mayst befriend me so much as to think   10
      I come one way of the Plantagenets.

HUBERT Unkind remembrance, thou and eyeless night
      Have done me shame. Brave soldier, pardon me
      That any accent breaking from thy tongue
      Should 'scape the true acquaintance of mine ear.   15

BASTARD Come, come; sans compliment, what news abroad?

Hubert reports that John has been poisoned by a monk. At the request of his son, Prince Henry, John has pardoned the barons. The Bastard has lost half his army, caught by the tide.

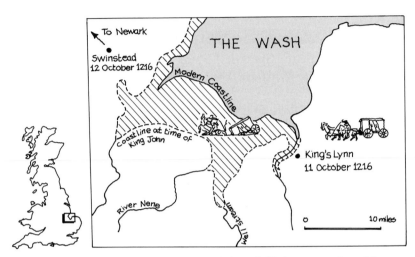

'These Lincoln Washes have devourèd them.' Shakespeare alters history again. It was King John, not the Bastard, who lost his baggage-train in the Wash. John's accident happened as he travelled from King's Lynn to Swinstead (Swineshead). He died at Newark during his campaigns against the barons, who challenged his rejection of Magna Carta.

No one knows the exact route John took. The coastline has changed since John's time. Today, people are still searching for John's treasure.

1 'A resolvèd villain'

The monk who poisoned King John tasted the same meal and died: his 'bowels … burst out'. No one can be sure if the story is true. John may simply have contracted dysentery from his exhausting military campaigning. From what you have learned about John so far, how likely do you think the poisoning story is?

---

swound swoon
broke out left
sudden time emergency
How did … taste to him? who tasted his food? (kings had food-tasters, who ate first to detect poison)

peradventure perhaps
tend look after
bear overreach, aspire

HUBERT Why here walk I in the black brow of night
        To find you out.
BASTARD   Brief then; and what's the news?
HUBERT O my sweet sir, news fitting to the night,
        Black, fearful, comfortless, and horrible.   20
BASTARD Show me the very wound of this ill news.
        I am no woman, I'll not swound at it.
HUBERT The king, I fear, is poisoned by a monk.
        I left him almost speechless and broke out
        To acquaint you with this evil, that you might   25
        The better arm you to the sudden time
        Than if you had at leisure known of this.
BASTARD How did he take it? Who did taste to him?
HUBERT A monk, I tell you, a resolvèd villain,
        Whose bowels suddenly burst out. The king   30
        Yet speaks and peradventure may recover.
BASTARD Who didst thou leave to tend his majesty?
HUBERT Why, know you not? The lords are all come back,
        And brought Prince Henry in their company,
        At whose request the king hath pardoned them,   35
        And they are all about his majesty.
BASTARD Withhold thine indignation, mighty heaven,
        And tempt us not to bear above our power!
        I'll tell thee, Hubert, half my power this night,
        Passing these flats, are taken by the tide.   40
        These Lincoln Washes have devourèd them,
        Myself, well mounted, hardly have escaped.
        Away before; conduct me to the king.
        I doubt he will be dead or ere I come.
                                                    Exeunt

Prince Henry reports that John is near to death, and orders him to be brought into the open air. Prince Henry reflects on the way in which John sings on his deathbed.

1 New set, new character

a Design the set for this final scene, which takes place in the orchard of Swinstead Abbey.

b Prince Henry was actually only eleven years old at the time of King John's death. Decide what age you think Shakespeare makes Prince Henry appear to be in this scene. What age would you make him in your own production?

2 Reflections on death

Prince Henry says that when suffering is very acute, it ceases to be felt (lines 13–14). Having disabled the body, Death moves in to attack the mind, creating all kinds of delusions (lines 15–20). In that last period before death, King John sings, just as a dying swan was also supposed to sing (lines 20–4).

a No one is certain whether Shakespeare wrote 'insensible', 'invincible', 'invisible', 'unusable' or 'incurable' in line 16. Each might be possible. Decide, with reasons, which word you think is the most appropriate.

b What was it that John sang as he waited for death? Write a few snatches of what he may have sung. Your lines should reflect some experiences that John recalls, however fragmentary their nature. Think about the 'legions of strange fantasies' that attack John's mind as he approaches death.

---

touched corruptibly infected incurably
idle comments strange remarks
allay lessen, alleviate
fell deadly
siege attack

throng and press crowding in
hold stronghold (the mind)
Confound destroy
cygnet young swan
doleful sad

ACT 5 SCENE 7
The orchard of Swinstead Abbey

Enter PRINCE HENRY, SALISBURY and BIGOT

PRINCE HENRY It is too late. The life of all his blood
    Is touched corruptibly, and his pure brain
    (Which some suppose the soul's frail dwelling-house)
    Doth by the idle comments that it makes
    Foretell the ending of mortality.   5

Enter PEMBROKE

PEMBROKE His highness yet doth speak, and holds belief
    That being brought into the open air,
    It would allay the burning quality
    Of that fell poison which assaileth him.
PRINCE HENRY Let him be brought into the orchard here.   10
                             [*Exit Bigot*]
    Doth he still rage?
PEMBROKE   He is more patient
    Than when you left him; even now he sung.
PRINCE HENRY O vanity of sickness! Fierce extremes
    In their continuance will not feel themselves.
    Death, having preyed upon the outward parts,   15
    Leaves them insensible, and his siege is now
    Against the mind, the which he pricks and wounds
    With many legions of strange fantasies,
    Which in their throng and press to that last hold,
    Confound themselves. 'Tis strange that Death should sing.   20
    I am the cygnet to this pale faint swan,
    Who chants a doleful hymn to his own death,
    And from the organ-pipe of frailty sings
    His soul and body to their lasting rest.

Salisbury says Prince Henry will restore order to England. John is brought in, and he describes how the poison burns him inwardly, without relief. The Bastard arrives in haste.

'Within me is a hell.' King John's language is filled with images of heat and burning: hot summer (line 30), burning paper (lines 32–4), burned bosom (line 39), parched lips (line 40), hot salt tears (line 45), fiery torments of hell from poison (lines 46–8) and burnt ship-ropes (line 52). Consider each image in turn, and try to conjure up a picture in your mind to express it.

1 Humour in death: 'ill fare'

King John puns on Prince Henry's question, 'How fares your majesty?' (line 34). 'Fares' could mean 'eats' or 'goes'. John replies, 'Poisoned – ill fare'. Advise John how he should speak 'ill fare' (bitterly, ironically?). Say what the pun suggests to you about his character.

set a form ... rude bring order out of disorder
marry indeed (by Saint Mary)
maw throat or stomach
the north the north wind

strait mean, miserly
virtue power
unreprievable unpardonable
scalded ... motion in a hot sweat from frantic hurry

SALISBURY Be of good comfort, prince, for you are born   25
        To set a form upon that indigest
        Which he hath left so shapeless and so rude.

     JOHN *brought in* [*on a litter by* BIGOT *and attendants*]

KING JOHN Ay, marry, now my soul hath elbow-room,
        It would not out at windows nor at doors.
        There is so hot a summer in my bosom   30
        That all my bowels crumble up to dust.
        I am a scribbled form, drawn with a pen
        Upon a parchment, and against this fire
        So I shrink up.
PRINCE HENRY   How fares your majesty?
KING JOHN Poisoned – ill fare – dead, forsook, cast off,   35
        And none of you will bid the winter come
        To thrust his icy fingers in my maw,
        Nor let my kingdom's rivers take their course
        Through my burned bosom, nor entreat the north
        To make his bleak winds kiss my parchèd lips   40
        And comfort me with cold. I do not ask you much,
        I beg cold comfort; and you are so strait
        And so ungrateful, you deny me that.
PRINCE HENRY O that there were some virtue in my tears,
        That might relieve you!
KING JOHN   The salt in them is hot.   45
        Within me is a hell, and there the poison
        Is, as a fiend, confined to tyrannise
        On unreprievable, condemnèd blood.

     Enter BASTARD [*and* HUBERT]

BASTARD O, I am scalded with my violent motion
        And spleen of speed to see your majesty.   50

John, very close to death, says he lives only to hear the Bastard's news. He dies hearing of danger and disaster. The Bastard urges the barons to arms, but Salisbury tells that peace is near.

1 John's last moments

a King John's final words. John, knowing that death is very near, sees himself as a ship whose ropes ('tackle') are burnt, and whose rigging ('shrouds') is now only a single thread. He will become only a 'module' (counterfeit or mere image) of a king. Think about lines 51–8. Might there be pauses at particular points? Would certain words be emphasised? Write notes to guide the actor.

b The Bastard's tone. How does the Bastard, usually bluff and direct, speak to the dying king? Is he tactful, blunt, distraught or embarrassed? Experiment to find a suitable tone for lines 59–64.

c *'The King dies.'* Shakespeare left no indication as to just where and how John died. A stage convention has grown up that he dies after the Bastard's report of the approach of Lewis and the loss of the English troops in the Wash. Work out how and when John would die in your production. Whatever you decide, justify it on grounds of dramatic effect and your view of John's character.

2 'Stars' = barons

The Bastard speaks lines 74–80 to the barons, who have returned to King John. Because they have renewed their loyalty ('mended faiths'), he likens them to stars that now 'move in your right spheres', or planets that are now in their proper orbits. The image is one that Shakespeare drew upon in other plays: proper order in society reflects order in nature. See, for example, *Troilus and Cressida*, Act 1 Scene 3, lines 85–124: 'The heavens themselves …'.

---

set mine eye close my eyes after death
stay it by support my heart
confounded defeated
power army
upon advantage after a military success

you stars you barons
mended faiths renewed loyalties (of the barons)
respect self-respect
presently to leave immediately to end

KING JOHN O cousin, thou art come to set mine eye.
    The tackle of my heart is cracked and burnt,
    And all the shrouds wherewith my life should sail
    Are turnèd to one thread, one little hair.
    My heart hath one poor string to stay it by,   55
    Which holds but till thy news be utterèd,
    And then all this thou seest is but a clod
    And module of confounded royalty.
BASTARD The Dauphin is preparing hitherward,
    Where God He knows how we shall answer him,   60
    For in a night the best part of my power,
    As I upon advantage did remove,
    Were in the Washes all unwarily
    Devourèd by the unexpected flood.
              [The King dies]
SALISBURY You breathe these dead news in as dead an ear.   65
    My liege, my lord! – But now a king, now thus.
PRINCE HENRY Even so must I run on, and even so stop.
    What surety of the world, what hope, what stay,
    When this was now a king and now is clay?
BASTARD Art thou gone so? I do but stay behind   70
    To do the office for thee of revenge,
    And then my soul shall wait on thee to heaven,
    As it on earth hath been thy servant still. –
    Now, now, you stars that move in your right spheres,
    Where be your powers? Show now your mended faiths,   75
    And instantly return with me again
    To push destruction and perpetual shame
    Out of the weak door of our fainting land.
    Straight let us seek, or straight we shall be sought;
    The Dauphin rages at our very heels.   80
SALISBURY It seems you know not then so much as we.
    The Cardinal Pandulph is within at rest,
    Who half an hour since came from the Dauphin,
    And brings from him such offers of our peace
    As we with honour and respect may take,   85
    With purpose presently to leave this war.

Salisbury reports that Lewis's army is already leaving. Pandulph will negotiate peace. The Bastard orders John's funeral. All swear loyalty to Prince Henry. The Bastard proclaims England's invincibility.

1 The Bastard takes charge (in small groups)

The Bastard now seems to be the person with most authority in England. He is the son of Richard Cœur-de-lion. He is certain about the strength of his forces (line 88). Salisbury defers to him ('If you think meet' = If you agree). At his moment of greatest power, the Bastard voluntarily acknowledges Prince Henry as the legitimate king ('lineal state' = true inheritance) and submits to him, swearing his faithful service. The Bastard's final words are a rallying cry for the unity of England.

a Two versions: the Bastard might feel he could successfully seize the throne because of his military power, and call on his father's fame to uphold his claim. Work out two ways of performing lines 87–105. In the first, the Bastard willingly submits to Prince Henry and is truly patriotic. In the second, he makes the audience fully aware that he has strong thoughts of making a bid for the throne. Which version do you prefer? Why?

b 'Three corners': line 116 refers to France, Spain, and the Papal lands where the Pope was ruler. Suggest some stage business the Bastard could perform, to make this clear to a modern audience.

c '*Exeunt*' (everyone leaves the stage): make a list of all the characters who are on the stage. Work out how you would have them leave the stage to express your understanding of the play. For example, how is King John's body taken off? With great ceremony or as an afterthought?

d Final image: what would be the very last thing the audience sees as the curtain falls on your production?

---

well-sinewèd strongly prepared
carriages military wagons
cause and quarrel case and grievance
post hurry
consummate ... happily end the negotiations satisfactorily

like tender similar offer
spot stain, blemish
but needful woe only appropriate mourning
been beforehand with already received (or already ended)
rue regret, feel sorrow

BASTARD He will the rather do it when he sees
            Ourselves well-sinewèd to our defence.
SALISBURY Nay, 'tis in a manner done already,
            For many carriages he hath dispatched   90
            To the sea-side and put his cause and quarrel
            To the disposing of the cardinal,
            With whom yourself, myself, and other lords
            If you think meet, this afternoon will post
            To consummate this business happily.   95
BASTARD Let it be so. – And you, my noble prince,
            With other princes that may best be spared,
            Shall wait upon your father's funeral.
PRINCE HENRY At Worcester must his body be interred,
            For so he willed it.
BASTARD   Thither shall it then,   100
            And happily may your sweet self put on
            The lineal state and glory of the land!
            To whom with all submission on my knee
            I do bequeath my faithful services
            And·true subjection everlasting. [*Kneels*]   105
SALISBURY And the like tender of our love we make
            To rest without a spot for evermore.
                        [*Lords kneel*]
PRINCE HENRY I have a kind soul that would give thanks,
            And knows not how to do it but with tears.
BASTARD [*Rising*] O, let us pay the time but needful woe,   110
            Since it hath been beforehand with our griefs.
            This England never did, nor never shall,
            Lie at the proud foot of a conqueror,
            But when it first did help to wound itself.
            Now these her princes are come home again,   115
            Come the three corners of the world in arms,
            And we shall shock them. Nought shall make us rue,
            If England to itself do rest but true.
                                        Exeunt

Looking back at the play
Activities for groups or individuals

1 Patriotism: another anachronism

The Bastard's ringing patriotic call at the end of Act 5 is yet another of the play's anachronisms. The repudiation of foreigners is ironic. The Plantagenets, who came from Anjou (see pages 2–3), were hardly English. Neither were the Normans before them. At the time of King John, English was not the language of the ruling class. The first parliament to be conducted in English was still over 150 years away.

The legend of Robin Hood makes clear the subordinate position of the English in their own country at this time. The 'Englishmen' who were against 'bad King John' took to the woods to fight against the oppression of their foreign overlords. The Bastard would have been seen as one of those foreigners! You will find information on pages 176–8 which helps to explain why *King John* is a 'patriotic' play (because it was written in the England of Queen Elizabeth I).

Imagine that one of Shakespeare's actors reminded him in rehearsal about the legend of Robin Hood. The actor says, 'Can you re-think the play to make sure the viewpoint of the English people of the time is represented?' Shakespeare agrees, saying he will sketch out a couple of pages suggesting how it might be done. Write the first draft of Shakespeare's ideas.

2 Time and place in Act 5

List all the events in the seven scenes of Act 5. Suggest how much time elapses between each action. Decide how you would stage the seven scenes, to make the action flow without break on stage, but making clear the differences in location and time.

3 Loyalty ———————————————— Treachery

Draw a long line with 'Loyalty' at one end, and 'Treachery' at the other. Use the list of characters on page 1 to place each character at an appropriate point on your scale. Compare your placings with those of other students and talk together about differences. (You will probably wish to argue about 'loyal to whom?')

4 Update?

You have been invited to stage *King John*, and to set it in a time and place other than medieval England. How will you do it?

'Come the three corners of the world in arms, / And we shall shock them.'
The Bastard ends the play with a patriotic assertion of England's
invincibility. Imagine that the Bastard stays behind after everyone else
has left the stage. Write an epilogue for him to deliver, in which he speaks
his private thoughts to the audience. Will his private thoughts match
his public rhetoric?

What is *King John* about?

As always with Shakespeare, there is no single answer to the question 'what is the play about?' You can follow the story by reading the summaries of the action at the top of each left-hand page of this edition. These two pages offer other ways of understanding *King John*.

1 A history play

Shakespeare's portrayal of an historical period links together King John's three struggles:

a The wars with Arthur and King Philip over John's right to rule.

b The dispute with the Pope about religious authority.

c The quarrel with his barons.

2 A play of character

This perspective views the play as a study of men and women caught up in moral dilemmas. Certain characters gain or lose personal integrity under the stresses imposed by a world of power politics:

a King John dwindles from brave defiance of his enemies to abject submission to Rome. Like Lewis the Dauphin, he changes from a confident and noble man to an untrustworthy schemer. Earlier interpretations portrayed John as a Protestant hero, courageously resisting the demands of the Pope.

b The Bastard changes from a devil-may-care, plain-spoken madcap to a political and military realist. As he becomes a powerful military leader, he moves from cynicism to committed loyalty.

c Constance changes from vituperative would-be queen to grief-stricken mother. Arthur is often seen in two ways: as a sentimental, two-dimensional character, or as a poignant figure who appeals strongly to the audience's humanity and pity.

d Hubert appears loyal to John, but he breaks his oath to kill Arthur. His humanity and integrity contrast strongly with the self-interest (Commodity) which motivates other characters.

e Salisbury breaks his oath of loyalty, but eventually returns to the English side. Is he a hypocrite, or a deeply troubled and sincere man?

3 An exploration of politics and morality

The struggles between King John and his enemies can be seen as conflicts between different beliefs about right and wrong. The play is both a study in usurpation, and a comment on the nature of good government. As such, it embodies particular themes or principles:

Power versus justice (might versus right) How John defends, by force, his dubious claim to possession of the English crown. The play begins with Eleanor reminding John of the legal weakness of his claim to kingship: 'Your strong possession much more than your right'. At Angiers, the rightful king is to be decided by whoever wins the battle.

Commodity versus honesty How self-interest and devious behaviour lie behind talk of 'honour', 'right' and 'truth'. Both Pandulph's arguments and the Bastard's soliloquising on Commodity can be seen as machiavellian. (Machiavelli's *Il Principe* (The Prince), published in 1513, argued that any means, however deceitful, could be used by a ruler to maintain power. This ran counter to the traditional belief that, for the Christian monarch, honesty was the best policy.)

Treachery versus loyalty The breaking of faith and sworn promises. In a play where loyalty to king or country or ideal ('honour') is so prevalent, many characters break the vows they have made: John, King Philip, the barons, Lewis, Melun and Hubert. Patriotism and personal loyalties are called severely into question throughout the play.

4 A play of symmetries and parallels

The play has a highly patterned structure. Symmetries and parallels can be found throughout:

a Treachery, disloyalty or oath-breaking by many characters.

b Decline and growth. As King John 'falls', the Bastard rises.

c Disputed inheritance. Act 1 mirrors and forecasts the following acts. Both inheritance disputes involve a will, possession, right and power.

d Mothers and sons. Eleanor and John, Lady Falconbridge and the Bastard, and Constance and Arthur.

e The contrast of a golden age with a shabby age (the reign of Richard Cœur-de-lion versus that of King John).

Cast yourself as a character and tell the story of *King John* from your character's point of view.

History, legend and drama

History

King John was born in 1167. He was known as 'Lackland', because, as the youngest son of King Henry II, he had very few territories. John conspired against his own brother, Richard Cœur-de-lion, trying to seize his throne whilst Richard was held captive by the Duke of Austria. John became King of England in 1199, after Richard's death. During his reign, he lost most of his French territories to King Philip II of France (who supported Arthur's claim to the English throne).

John was excommunicated in 1209 because he refused to accept Stephen Langton as the Archbishop of Canterbury. The sentence of excommunication was lifted in 1213, when John surrendered his kingdom to the Pope's authority.

John's barons were enraged by his incessant demands for money. To make him acknowledge their rights, they compelled John to sign the Great Charter (Magna Carta) at Runnymede in 1215. Shortly afterwards, John repudiated the Charter, provoking the barons to rebel against him. During his campaigns against the barons, John fell ill and died at Newark in 1216.

Legend: villain and hero

John has the reputation of being an unpopular 'bad king'. The monks who first chronicled his life described him as a monster of depravity (but they may have been prejudiced by John's pillaging of the Church to pay for his many wars). He was portrayed as a tyrant: cruel, irreligious, lustful, hot-tempered, deceitful, superstitious and greedy. Legend says he killed Arthur with his own hands, in a drunken rage. John's love of hunting resulted in strict forest laws: death was the penalty for anyone cutting a branch from a tree in the king's forest. The legend of Robin Hood portrays John as a foreign overlord with these negative characteristics.

The Elizabethans created a different legend. They turned John into a Protestant hero, because of his defiance of the Pope. Historians today present a more balanced view of John, acknowledging his vices and failures, but recognising him as a skilled administrator, a brave military strategist and a notable judge.

Drama

Shakespeare was a dramatist, not an historian. His imagination worked on what he read about King John in Elizabethan history books, mainly Ralph Holinshed's *Chronicles of England, Scotland and Ireland* (1587). Shakespeare may also have been influenced by an earlier play, *The Troublesome Reign of John King of England*, published in 1591. This crudely written, virulently anti-Catholic play closely resembles *King John* in its characters, scenes and speech sequences. Shakespeare freely altered history for dramatic effect. He:

- invented the character of the Bastard and the whole of Act 1
- changed Arthur to a young and helpless boy
- created Austria from two historical figures: Austria, who imprisoned King Richard I, and Limoges (who killed Richard)
- shifted the death of John from Newark to Swinstead Abbey
- had John poisoned by a monk (he probably died of dysentery)
- added anachronisms: cannons, handkerchiefs (see pages 6 and 100).

| The struggle with Arthur (1199–1203). | The quarrel with the Pope (1207–1214). | The 'Barons' Revolt' and Magna Carta (1215). |

King John includes the three major conflicts of John's reign. But Shakespeare interwove the three events, which occurred at very different times. For example, he made the death of Arthur a prime cause of the revolt of the barons and the invasion of the French. In fact, Arthur died years before the barons rebelled and the French landed.

The relevance of *King John*

King John is very much a 'play for today'. Shakespeare's imaginative and dramatic re-working of early thirteenth-century history illuminates both Elizabethan England and our modern world.

King John and the England of Elizabeth I

King John was a familiar figure to the first Elizabethans. Every Sunday, in church, Shakespeare's contemporaries listened to the 'Homily against Disobedience'. It held up John's reign as an example of the disasters that resulted when a monarch's rule was challenged. John was seen as an early Protestant martyr. He nearly succeeded in breaking with Roman Catholicism, a feat finally accomplished over 300 years later by Queen Elizabeth's father, King Henry VIII. Elizabethans saw strong parallels between John and Elizabeth:

a The threat from Roman Catholicism. Both John and Elizabeth:
  - were regarded as illegitimate rulers by Rome
  - defied the Pope's claim to spiritual authority over England
  - were excommunicated (see page 68)
  - were put under the death sentence by the Pope
  - experienced assassination attempts (for example, by poison).

b The threat to succession (the right to rule). Both monarchs:
  - faced many challenges to their right to the English throne
  - based their legitimate right to succeed on a disputed will
  - were called usurpers
  - caused rivals to be killed (Arthur and Mary, Queen of Scots)
  - blamed a subordinate for the rival claimants' deaths. The scapegoats were Hubert and Davison.

c Internal and external enemies. Both Elizabeth and John:
  - faced challenges to their authority from their own nobles
  - had Spain as a common enemy
  - faced invasion by a foreign power
  - learned that the invaders plotted to kill their English allies
  - heard of the wreck, off the English coast, of invasion fleets (John, the Goodwin Sands; Elizabeth, the Armada of 1588).

Contemporary relevance

King John

King John has particular relevance for today. The play has no clear heroes; mercenaries flock to fight for dubious causes; innocents are helpless victims of political intrigues; treaties are made and broken; there is treachery at all levels. The tone and mood of our own contemporary world (and of a good deal of modern literature) are reflected in the play: the inconclusive ending, the many ironies, the sardonic commentaries of the Bastard, the anguished language of women and men caught up in an ever-shifting world which lacks security.

Politics

In its portrayal of politics, *King John* uncomfortably mirrors contemporary affairs. Today, as then, factional groups struggle for power, seeking to create new nations, desperate for territory and intolerant of all opposition. As Pandulph pronounces the Pope's death sentence on King John, there is a sombre prediction of modern state terrorism.

Self-interest: 'Commodity'

The play's exposure of 'Commodity' and 'policy' provides illuminating insights into the double-dealings of public life today, where self-interest, short-term gain and the sleaziness of always having an eye to the main chance are often evident. The machiavellianism (see page 175) which Shakespeare so sharply lays bare in *King John* is as much alive today as it was then.

Rhetoric

King John abounds in the dubious use of persuasive language: the bombastic assertion and the threatenings of the kings before Angiers; the slippery casuistry of Pandulph; the evasive and crafty way in which King John persuades Hubert to murder Arthur; the language of public relations in the Bastard's spurious descriptions of John.

Patriotism and nationalism

The play provides troubling insights into 'patriotism' and 'nationalism', ideologies regarded by some with deepest scepticism, by others with uncritical acceptance. In *King John*, patriotism to England is put under the microscope, but the issues and arguments have a wider application. In the modern world, every nation seeks to ensure the allegiance and commitment of its citizens, by appeals to patriotism or nationalism.

King John and the Bastard

John's decline

King John's character and language change through the play. He begins as a courageous military commander, stoutly defying the demands of France and Rome. But with the capture of Arthur, his devious nature becomes clear. His language to Hubert is ambiguous and evasive, as he seeks the boy's death. He collapses into nervous cowardice and fear as the barons revolt, and he abjectly submits to the Pope. Ineffectual and sick, he hands command of the English army to the Bastard. He dies at Swinstead Abbey, tortured by the poison that burns within him, but with no words of repentance or remorse. His 'progress' from hero to corrupt coward can be shown as follows:

A bold proud king defending the Angevin Empire: 'Here have we war for war and blood for blood,/Controlment for control' (Act 1 Scene 1, lines 19–20).

An intrepid military tactician moving swiftly to attack King Philip and his allies at Angiers: 'His marches are expedient to this town,/His forces strong, his soldiers confident' (Act 2 Scene 1, lines 60–1).

An unscrupulous politician exchanging half a kingdom for a crown, as he gives away five provinces to Lewis (Act 2 Scene 1, lines 527–30).

A Protestant hero defiantly rejecting the Pope's demands: 'Yet I alone, alone do me oppose/Against the Pope and count his friends my foes' (Act 3 Scene 1, lines 170–1).

A shifty child-murderer as he orders Arthur's execution: 'Death ... A grave ... Enough' (Act 3 Scene 3, line 66).

A weak, submissive king yielding to the authority of the Pope, as he hands over the crown: 'Thus have I yielded up into your hand/The circle of my glory' (Act 5 Scene 1, lines 1–2).

A guilt-ridden conscience 'O, my heart is sick' (Act 5 Scene 3, line 4).

A dying man tortured by the pain of poison 'I beg cold comfort; and you are so strait/And so ungrateful' (Act 5 Scene 7, lines 42–3).

Trace John's progress through the play, collecting quotations which illustrate the outline above.

The Bastard: mad-cap, Machiavel, military leader

The Bastard can be viewed as a descendant of the Vice of medieval plays, and the Machiavel of Elizabethan drama. Such characters delighted in their own slyness, humorously confiding in the audience, and poking fun at rank and status. Shakespeare uses the Bastard to acknowledge the theatricality of events, and he compares the citizens of Angiers to an audience watching a play: 'As in a theatre, whence they gape and point / At your industrious scenes and acts of death'.

But the ebullient Bastard is a complex character, who grows in understanding and moral stature. His development can be seen as a political coming of age in four stages:

Act 1 the devil-may-care mad-cap. His language is jaunty, full of bravado. He is wittily off-hand to royalty, speaking his mind plainly. Newly created a knight, he mockingly apes the manners of the nobility, and flatters his way to enhance his social position.

Act 2 the ironic commentator. The Bastard's asides, military advice and soliloquy show his growing political awareness. Having seen the self-interested political bargainings of two kings, he cynically decides to follow their example and make gain his own goal.

Acts 3 and 4 from revenger and plunderer to puzzled observer. The Bastard mocks and kills Austria, his father's killer. He goes willingly to ransack the English abbeys in order to fill King John's war coffers. But the death of Arthur causes him to reflect with amazement on the confusions of the times.

Act 5 military leader and patriot. The Bastard is the voice of authority, using heroic language to try to lift John's spirits and to challenge the French. He becomes the undisputed leader of the English forces. A committed patriot, he ends the play with a clarion call for the unity of England.

a Use the descriptions above to review the Bastard's progress through the play. Pay particular attention to the soliloquies or speeches with which he closes Acts 1, 2, 4 and 5. Collect lines or phrases which illustrate the different stages of the Bastard's development.

b John's fall, the Bastard's rise. Draw a diagram to show how John declines during the play and how the Bastard rises.

The language of *King John*

1 Personification

Throughout *King John*, Shakespeare turns all kinds of things or abstractions into persons, giving them parts of the human body:

white-faced shore	foot of peace	rumour's tongue
deep-mouthed thunder	face of right	wall-eyed wrath
drowsy ear of night	proud foot	hand of time
broad-eyed watchful day	welkin's ear	fat ribs of peace
beauteous eye of heaven	eyeless night	hand of nature

Sometimes, he gives them human expression or feelings:

churlish drums	lusty trumpet	coward hand
hot malicious day	tyrant fever	stern occasion
sweet world's taste	cannon's malice	confused wrong
unacquainted change	fainting land	stumbling night

Human feelings themselves are personified: soft remorse, hasty spleen, wild amazement, bragging horror, staring rage, Misery's love, bitter shame. The besieged city of Angiers is given many human attributes: 'eyes', 'cheeks', 'ears', 'waist', 'flinty ribs', 'bosom'. The city is described as 'winking', 'sleeping', 'peevish', and threatened with 'shaking fever'.

Memorable and sustained personifications stand out:

War 'dogged war', 'gallant head of war', 'dwarfish war', 'tongue of war', 'wings of war', 'grappling vigour and rough frown of war'.

Death 'The swords of soldiers are his teeth, his fangs', 'the rotten carcass of old Death', 'amiable, lovely Death', ''Tis strange that Death should sing'.

Grief 'Grief is proud and makes his owner stoop', 'Grief fills the room up of my absent child,/Lies in his bed, walks up and down with me'.

Commodity (self-interest) 'that sly devil ... That daily break-vow ... That smooth-faced gentleman'.

The illustration on the cover of this edition is Albrecht Dürer's drawing of Death as the fourth Horseman of the Apocalypse. It is set against a fourteenth-century picture of King John hunting. Design your own cover illustration for an edition of *King John*, inspired by one or more of the personifications above.

2 Imagery

a The body

King John is rich in images of the human body (tongue, ear, head, and so on). Sometimes, the human body is an analogy for the 'body politic' (the state or nation; for example, England): 'The body of this fleshly land'. Sometimes, the 'body image' creates a vivid picture: 'bare-ribbed Death', 'the cannons have their bowels full of wrath', 'that white-faced shore,/Whose foot spurns back the ocean's roaring tide'.

Many of the 'body images' suggest some violence against the body or the state: 'We from the west will send destruction/Into this city's bosom'. At other times, Shakespeare's reference to the body is quite literal: 'Why then I suck my teeth'.

On every page of this edition, there is at least one 'body image' (for example, 'blood', 'foot', 'eye'). Some pages have many such images. Turn back to any three pages at random. Identify the body images on each page, and talk together about how each image helps to enrich the meaning of the lines at that point. Find a vivid way of illustrating your findings (for example, by drawing the outline of a human body and entering each quotation on it).

b Speed and heat

In real life, King John was hot-tempered and hasty. He was constantly on the move to attempt to quell the many military challenges he faced throughout his reign. Shakespeare frequently uses imagery of speed and heat (particularly 'fire') in *King John*.

In Act 1, John claims he will move faster than lightning to fight with France. In Act 4 Scene 1, heat images climax dramatically, with the threat to burn out Arthur's eyes. Act 5, like a quick-flowing film script, moves rapidly from place to place, and from action to action. John leaves the battlefield at Bury St Edmunds, regretting how 'this tyrant fever burns me up' (Act 5 Scene 3, line 14). He dies at Swinstead Abbey with 'so hot a summer in my bosom', begging to be comforted with cold to relieve the fire within, that causes him to shrink like a parchment held to a flame.

Find between four and six lines or phrases from different parts of the play which call up pictures of heat or speed in your imagination. Use them to write a poem (or paragraph) of between ten and twenty lines about John, entitled, 'Fiery swiftness'.

3 Key words: 'right' and 'hand'

Because the play deals with the struggle to rule territory, it is not surprising that the words 'King', 'France' and 'England' are often used (the last two standing for both kings and countries). But two other words, 'right' (or 'rights') and 'hand', echo throughout the play. Both occur in *King John* more times that in any other Shakespeare play:

Right In the first forty lines of the play, 'right' is used five times. It pinpoints a key issue: who has the legal right to rule?

Hand In this edition, the word 'hand' occurs over seventy times. Sometimes, it is used literally or as a stage direction ('What means that hand upon that breast of thine?'). Sometimes, it is used as an image of power or of a treaty ('Thus have I yielded up into your hand,/The circle of my glory'). At yet other times, it is used as a personification ('Fortune ... with her golden hand hath plucked on France'). Nearly every use of 'hand' carries a symbolism deeper than its surface meaning.

Trace either 'right' or 'hand' through the play. *Either* write an essay *or* make a display of your findings, to illustrate how your chosen word embodies a major theme (or themes) of the play.

4 The language of perplexity

A sense of amazement and incredulity runs through *King John*. Expressions of perplexity identify personal, moral and political dilemmas:

- The Bastard's words on Arthur's death: 'I am amazed, methinks, and lose my way/Among the thorns and dangers of this world'.
- King Philip's: 'I am perplexed and know not what to say', as Pandulph demands he break from King John.
- Blanche's agonised: 'which is the side that I must go withal?', as she is forced to choose between her new husband and her family .
- Constance's many incredulous questions, as she hears of the marriage of Blanche and Lewis and the dispossession of her son.
- Arthur's disbelief that Hubert intends to put out his eyes.

Consider each major character in turn, and identify one or two occasions when they use the language of perplexity. Design a diagram entitled 'the moral maze', to present your quotations.

5 Blank verse

Elizabethans watching a play did not expect the actors to speak in everyday language. The convention was that plays (especially history plays) should be written in verse. This fulfilled expectations that the characters' language would be 'poetic'. Verse has the formal, ceremonious rhythm felt to be particularly suitable for kings and for great affairs of war and state.

King John is written entirely in verse. The style is mainly blank verse (unrhymed), but very occasionally Shakespeare uses rhyme. Each ten-syllable line of blank verse has five alternating unstressed (x) and stressed (/) syllables (iambic pentameter), as in the first and last lines of the play:

```
 x   /   x  /  x   /   x     /     x   /
```
Now say, Chatillon, what would France with us?

```
x  /   x  /  x /  x  /   x   /
```
If England to itself do rest but true

The rhythm makes the lines easier to learn. The danger of blank verse is that it can sound boringly repetitive if it is spoken very mechanically. But it is a very flexible style (some people say it is close to the natural rhythm of human speech). Actors always try to ensure that blank verse does not sound stilted on stage.

A line is often shaped into two halves, with a mid-line pause (caesura) and an end-of-line pause (end-stopping). Often a line 'makes sense' on its own, but sometimes one line will 'flow' into the next (enjambment or run-on line). *King John* is one of Shakespeare's earlier plays, and the verse is very regular (unlike *Macbeth*).

To experience the rhythm of iambic pentameter, read a few lines aloud from anywhere in the play, but pronounce each syllable very clearly, almost as if each one were a separate word. As you read, beat out the five-stress rhythm (clap hands, or tap your desk). Carry on practising speaking lines, taking account of the rhythm, but bringing out the meaning of the words as fully as you can. Talk together with a partner about how a good actor can use the underlying rhythm to reinforce and clarify meaning, without making the rhythm too obvious or boring.

Invent a few blank verse lines of your own, to create short scenes which are mentioned in the play, but not shown. For example, the Bastard ransacking the abbeys, or a soliloquy for a monk, as he prepares the poisoned food for King John.

6 Absent prose

There is no prose in *King John*. Shakespeare normally uses prose for comic scenes or for low-status characters. Invent a short scene in prose, in which two citizens (either French or English) talk together about all they have seen and heard about the doings of King John.

7 One-liners

- James Gurney speaks only four words (Act 1 Scene 1, line 231).
- Peter of Pomfret speaks only one line (Act 4 Scene 2, line 154).
- Essex speaks only three lines (Act 1 Scene 1, lines 44–6).
- The Executioner speaks only two lines (Act 4 Scene 1, lines 6 and 85).

Imagine that the actors playing these characters ask Shakespeare to give them more to say. Write a few lines for one character, to insert at appropriate points in the scene in which he appears.

8 Rhetoric: public language to persuade

King John is rich in rhetoric: language used to persuade others. The style is often bombastic and declamatory, full of boasts, threats and defiance. In Act 2, for example, King John and King Philip threaten the citizens of Angiers, using elaborate and pretentious words and phrases (Act 2 Scene 1, lines 204–66). The Citizen replies in kind, 'The sea enragèd is not half so deaf ...'. In Act 5, the Bastard praises John in a tone of heroic defiance (Act 5 Scene 2, lines 127–58). This ceremonial, blustering style is for public consumption. Its hyperbole (excessively exaggerated language) is intended to strike fear into enemies, and to put heart into friends and supporters.

Striking adjectives accompany nouns ('apish and unmannerly approach'). The language is regular, highly patterned and formal. Sound takes precedence over meaning. Such rhetoric is used by military leaders to inspire patriotism and warlike action. It is the language of the public platform, not that of informal conversation or reasoned argument.

Identify a passage of rhetoric in each of the five acts. Work out two ways to deliver each. First, to give your chosen passages full rhetorical effect. Second, to expose the insincerity and boastful qualities of the language (for example, by having an ironic commentator, or by mockingly repeating each hyperbolic word or phrase).

Staging *King John*

There is no record of a production of the play in Shakespeare's lifetime. But *King John* enjoyed much success in the eighteenth and nineteenth centuries. Productions became more and more elaborate. Designers created spectacular stagings of the medieval world through sets, costumes and props. Huge casts took part in epic enactments of battles and coronations. Invented scenes were inserted (the signing of Magna Carta was a favourite addition). In the twentieth century, productions took an increasingly sceptical stance towards patriotism and chivalry. Irony and harsh political relevance were emphasised. Small casts, simple staging and an awareness of the horrors of war, have produced memorable interpretations of *King John*.

Stage your own production of *King John*

Talk together about whether you would wish to 'update' *King John* (for example, with modern military uniforms), and how you might emphasise its relevance to the modern world. Then choose one or more of the following activities:

Design the set No one knows precisely where Shakespeare intended each scene to be set. This edition suggests locations at the beginning of each scene, but you can challenge them. Work out how you would depict Angiers, King John's palace, Bury St Edmunds and Swinstead Abbey (or your own suggested locations).

Design the costumes Look at the examples shown, then invent your own.

Design the props Begin with swords and crowns, and Hubert's hot irons. Think about whether you would give each character a distinctive prop (for example, one production gave the Bastard's mother a riding-whip which she used to great effect in her single appearance!).

Design the publicity poster Make people want to see your play!

Write character notes Many directors provide notes for the actors' guidance (pages 174–7 and 180–1 will help you).

Obtain funding Work out a five-minute presentation for potential sponsors. Convince them the that play can appeal to young people.

Cast the play From your class, or from well-known film or stage actors (give reasons for your choices).

William Shakespeare 1564–1616

1564 Born Stratford-upon-Avon, eldest son of John and Mary Shakespeare.
1582 Marries Anne Hathaway of Shottery, near Stratford.
1583 Daughter, Susanna, born.
1585 Twins, son and daughter, Hamnet and Judith, born.
1592 First mention of Shakespeare in London. Robert Greene, another playwright, described Shakespeare as 'an upstart crow beautified with our feathers …'. Greene seems to have been jealous of Shakespeare. He mocked Shakespeare's name, calling him 'the only Shake-scene in the country' (presumably because Shakespeare was writing successful plays).
1595 A shareholder in 'The Lord Chamberlain's Men', an acting company that became extremely popular.
1596 Son Hamnet dies, aged eleven.
     Father, John, granted arms (acknowledged as a gentleman).
1597 Buys New Place, the grandest house in Stratford.
1598 Acts in Ben Jonson's *Every Man in His Humour*.
1599 Globe Theatre opens on Bankside. Performances in the open air.
1601 Father, John, dies.
1603 James I grants Shakespeare's company a royal patent: 'The Lord Chamberlain's Men' became 'The King's Men' and played about twelve performances each year at court.
1607 Daughter, Susanna, marries Dr John Hall.
1608 Mother, Mary, dies.
1609 'The King's Men' begin performing indoors at Blackfriars Theatre.
1610 Probably returned from London to live in Stratford.
1616 Daughter, Judith, marries Thomas Quiney.
     Dies. Buried in Holy Trinity Church, Stratford-upon-Avon.

The plays and poems
(no one knows exactly when he wrote each play)

1589–1595 *The Two Gentlemen of Verona, The Taming of the Shrew, First, Second and Third Parts of King Henry VI, Titus Andronicus, King Richard III, The Comedy of Errors, Love's Labour's Lost, A Midsummer Night's Dream, Romeo and Juliet, King Richard II* (and the long poems *Venus and Adonis* and *The Rape of Lucrece*).

1596–1599 *King John, The Merchant of Venice, First and Second Parts of King Henry IV, The Merry Wives of Windsor, Much Ado About Nothing, King Henry V, Julius Caesar* (and probably the *Sonnets*).

1600–1605 *As You Like It, Hamlet, Twelfth Night, Troilus and Cressida, Measure for Measure, Othello, All's Well That Ends Well, Timon of Athens, King Lear*.

1606–1611 *Macbeth, Antony and Cleopatra, Pericles, Coriolanus, The Winter's Tale, Cymbeline, The Tempest*.

1613 *King Henry VIII, The Two Noble Kinsmen* (both probably with John Fletcher).

1623 Shakespeare's plays published as a collection (now called the First Folio).